SEX ROLES AND THE SCHOOL

Schools reflect the society which surrounds them, but they must also be agents of change. When first published, this book argued that, for a variety of reasons, schools and other educational institutions enforce a set of gender roles more rigid than those current in wider society, leading to a deceptive pattern of underachievement, particularly amongst working-class girls. The last decade has seen an explosion of research on gender and education and, in this completely updated edition of her ground-breaking text, Sara Delamont examines, in a rigorous but highly accessible way, new research findings and new strategies for change, continuing to argue that both sexes lose out from sexist schooling.

The book will appeal directly both to students and to experienced teachers wishing to update themselves on recent developments in the subject. It contains a great deal of theoretical and practical guidance, and is particularly useful for the classroom.

Sara Delamont is Reader in Sociology at the University of Wales College of Cardiff. Her books for Routledge include *Interaction in the Classroom, Knowledgeable Women* and, with Maurice Galton, *Inside the Secondary Classroom.*

EDUCATION IN SOCIETY SERIES
Series edited by Stephen J. Ball

SEX ROLES AND THE SCHOOL

2nd edition

Sara Delamont

London and New York

207561

First edition published 1980 by Methuen & Co. Ltd
Second edition published 1990
by Routledge
11 New Fetter Lane, London EC4P 4EE

Simultaneously published in the USA and Canada
by Routledge
a division of Routledge, Chapman and Hall, Inc.
29 West 35th Street, New York, NY 10001

© 1980, 1990 Sara Delamont
Typeset by Witwell Ltd, Southport
Printed in Great Britain by
T.J. Press (Padstow) Ltd, Padstow, Cornwall.

British Library Cataloguing in Publication Data
Delamont, Sara, *1947-*
    Sex roles and the school. — 2nd ed — (Education in
society)
    1. Great Britain. Schools. Students. Sex roles
    I. Title
    370.19345

    ISBN 0-415-03842-1

Library of Congress Cataloging in Publication Data
Delamont, Sara, 1947-
        Sex roles and the school/Sara Delamont.
            p.   cm. — (Education in society series)
        Includes bibliographical references.
        ISBN 0-415-03842-1 — ISBN 0-415-03843-X
(pbk.)
        1. Sex discrimination in education — Great Britain.
        2. Sex role—Great Britain. I. Title. II. Series.
LC212.3.G7D44   1990
370.19'345'0941—dc20   90-31602
                                                                              CIP

Contents

Series editor's preface

In pessimistic perspective, there is every danger that the pace and scope of recent educational reforms in Britain, especially the introduction of a National Curriculum and national testing, will have the effect of diverting attention and effort away from those aspects of the educational process which tend to debilitate and marginalize 50 per cent of our population – women. Optimistically, the shortage of skilled workers in the 1990s in sectors of the labour market where women have traditionally been excluded may have dramatic effects in terms of attempts by powerful, previously uninterested lobbies, to attract girls into boys' subjects, like science. Perhaps we shall see real reform for the wrong reasons. In terms of the amount of heat and noise produced by educational research, gender has been one of the biggest and busiest areas of activity in recent years. Unfortunately, up to now, in terms of real reform in schools, progress towards sex equality has been slow and limited. Sara Delamont's book demonstrates exactly why it is that such equality is so difficult to achieve, and also what needs to be done to achieve it. The book documents the variety of entrenched practices and assumptions in schools which support and reproduce gender bias.

Significantly, while the book is presented as a second edition of the author's earlier bestseller, the reader who compares this with the earlier text will find little repetition of material. The flow of research reported in the 1970s became a flood in the 1980s. This is an up-to-date and lively guide to that material organized around the key issues. The book is challenging to teachers, men and women, and to parents. It is a committed book but it is also practical and particularly relevant to the beginning teacher.

Stephen J. Ball

Preface and acknowledgements to the second edition

The original version of this book appeared in 1980 and was written in 1978 and 1979. Since then the research base has grown rapidly, and the relevant literature is now too large for any one scholar to grasp. The whole book has been substantially updated, and where possible research from the 1980s substituted for earlier studies. The thrust of the argument has not been changed, but the illustrations are new. Some themes have gone, and some issues are treated in less detail than before. Central to the book is the belief that sexism is a destructive force which harms both sexes, and so the education system should be infused with non-sexist values and practices.

The original edition was typed by Myrtle Robins. This one was word processed by Elizabeth Renton, Pat Harris and Jan O'Sullivan. The library staff of UWCC supported the research with professional dedication. Some of the data were gathered during projects funded by the ESRC (which employed Paul Croll, Anne Jasman, John Willcocks, Margaret Greig, Janice Lea and Sarah Tann, under the direction of Brian Simon and Maurice Galton) and the Welsh Education Office (which employed Frances Beasley and Jane Pilcher directed by Graham Upton and Teresa Rees). Staff and pupils in schools in three English towns (Ashburton, Bridgehampton and Coalthorpe), in Edinburgh and in South Wales have patiently suffered me lurking on the margins of their lives for twenty years with good grace.

Stephen Ball found a place for the second edition of this book in his new series for which I am grateful. Since 1980 my ideas on gender have been discussed with Anne Murcott, Teresa Rees, Jane Pilcher, Mary Darmanin, Rhian Ellis, Alka Malvankar and

Val Connors as well as various male colleagues. Paul Atkinson read the drafts of this version of the book with his usual fortitude and perception when he could have been doing his own work. I owe him an incalculable debt for his support, criticism and sociological imagination. He also word processed the bibliography for me, a true labour of Hercules.

In 1969 forty-four pupils at 'St Luke's' made me aware of issues surrounding gender and schooling. This new edition is dedicated to those women as they enter their thirty-fifth year, and to the memory of Professor Gillian M. Powell who died just as she was about to be the first woman deputy principal of UWCC. A staunch supporter of women's rights, she will be much missed.

Sara Delamont

1 Introduction

A recent school ethnography includes the following comment on women teachers:

> If you pushed me, yes, I'd have to say that women in my view do not on the whole make as effective teachers as men. But before the *Women's Guardian* sends someone to stone me, let me add that there are very many exceptions, including one or two here, and that I am talking in particular about working in *this* school. . . . This school is a large boys' school, the majority of the staff are men, and the ethos is male. Women often prove to be a liability.
>
> (Beynon 1985b:173)

On 7 June 1987, the *TV Times* Problem Page published the following letter:

> Name-callers
> I am a 13 year old boy at high school, and my problem is name-calling. I do not know why, but other children have started shouting 'gaylord' and 'fruity boy' at me, and I find it very upsetting. Can you please advise me how to cope with the strain?
> KK, Antrim, Northern Ireland

Issues of sex, gender and even sexuality are omnipresent in education systems. In these two quotes a male teacher tells John Beynon about his distrust of his female colleagues, in the second an adolescent boy reveals the peer pressures on male pupils to conform to certain standards of masculine behaviour. This volume explores the ways in which beliefs about sex and gender influence life in our schools, and, in turn, how school affects our beliefs about sex and gender.

It would be ridiculous to argue, or even imply, that schools create sex stereotyping against the trend of the wider society. Schools reflect the society in which they are embedded, and attempts to innovate which challenge the orthodoxy of the community around them often run into trouble (Smith *et al.* 1986, 1987, 1988, Gold and Miles 1981). Pupils are strongly influenced by their homes and neighbourhoods, and may discount what teachers and schoolbooks say. However, a body of research (Rutter *et al.* 1979, Mortimore *et al.* 1988) reveals that schools do influence pupils' lives and achievements, and those who wish to change society frequently look to education as their vehicle. Thus various groups in Britain look to education to prevent prejudice, stop pupils smoking, banish litter dropping, improve babycare, raise the level of political debate and bring about many other social changes. Campaigners for women's rights have been no exception to this and hope to use education to train girls for better jobs, prevent wife-battering and generally reduce *sexism* in society. (Sexism is a term meaning stereotyping people by sex, just as racism is stereotyping people by race.)

This book does *not* argue that schools create sex roles in boys and girls which are at odds with the sex roles operating in the wider society. However, it does argue that schools develop and reinforce sex segregations, stereotypes, and even discriminations which exaggerate the negative aspects of sex roles in the outside world, when they could be trying to alleviate them. There is sexism outside schools as the following extract shows:

> My brother and I are twins aged nearly sixteen. My mother wants me to leave school and wants my brother to stay on for a better education as she says girls don't need it – they get married. I'm very interested in French and am doing well in it at school. Do you think it is fair that I should have to leave and my brother stay on?
>
> (*TV Times* 3 July 1976)

The 'problem' was quoted at the end of the first edition of this book. There are still plenty of parents, teachers, heads, advisors, governors, employers and adolescents who hold sexist views and act in ways that discriminate against one sex or the other, without even being aware of what they are doing. The research that has been produced often fails to reach pre-service teachers, or those on in-service courses, and if it does reach them it does not convince them.

There are statistical studies of sex inequalities in education revealing the lack of girls in science and craft, design and technology (CDT) after the age of 14, and maths after 16, balanced by a lack of boys in foreign languages, home economics and office skills courses after 14. There are job vacancies for young people with skills, but the early evidence from research into the Technical and Vocational Education Initiative (TVEI) and Certificate of Pre-Vocational Education (CPVE) is that boys and girls are being offered *different* training and vocational preparation which is based on outmoded ideas that the labour market will stay sex segregated. Sceptical readers can easily find such statistics in the educational press and government publications. Here the emphasis is on the social relationships that continue every day in schools, where individual teachers can begin to change and challenge sex-role norms. Individual teachers can do little directly to alter the national statistical picture, but we can all change small things in the content and process of our lessons.

There are five main ways in which schools differentiate between boys and girls to the disadvantage of both sexes. These are: the organization of the school; the teacher's strategies for controlling and motivating pupils; the organization and content of lessons; the informal conversations between pupils and their teachers; and leaving unchallenged the pupils' own stereotyping and self-segregating of activities. In Britain's schools the sexes are still being segregated; the differences between males and females are highlighted and exaggerated; in some either males or females are being disadvantaged. The central arguments of this book are that schools should be actively concerned with sex equality, even if that means confronting stereotyped beliefs pupils hold. Many aspects of everyday life in schools shown in this book should not be happening.

In general, the higher the attainment level of pupils the less sex differentiation there is in their curriculum. There are examples of sex stereotyping in sixth forms (e.g. Stanworth 1983) and top bands, but the process is much more blatant and explicit in industrial training units for slow learners (Shone and Atkinson 1981), in Youth Training Schemes (YTS) (Brelsford *et al.* 1982, Rees 1983, Cockburn 1987)and in the remedial classes of comprehensive schools (Burgess 1983, 1988, 1989). It is easier for a clever pupil to opt for an unusual subject choice or career than for a low-ability pupil, or one who is already in rebellion against the school, or one who is not achieving academic success. The other four types of sex differentiation bear on pupils of all achievement levels with equal force (Delamont 1980b, 1982, 1983a, b, 1984a, b, 1986). The evidence that schools are places where a great deal of unthinking sex discrimination goes on is examined in this book.

The consequences of sex differentiation and sex discrimination

The consequences of sex differentiation are slightly different for boys and girls. The boy who goes through school looking down on females, being allowed to adhere to the sexual double standard, unable to cook and sew, ignorant of childcare and equipped for a world where women wait on his emotional and domestic needs is handicapped for his future family and domestic life, and a lost cause for sexual responsibility and parenthood. He is primarily disadvantaged in his personal, emotional and home life. The girl who does not learn to assert herself, has not studied science, technology and 'heavy' craft is primarily handicapped in the labour market, because she lacks the skills (or confidence to acquire them) which lead to higher-paying jobs. However, both sexes are disadvantaged in both domestic and employment spheres if their schooling has left their ideas about sex roles unchallenged and trapped in traditional stereotypes. Boys will be unwilling to enter occupations that are associated with women, even if such jobs (e.g. in the catering and retailing industries) are expanding. Girls will face unhappy home lives if the men they marry are domestically incompetent and hold different expectations about marriage from their own.

This may seem to be an exaggerated, even hysterical, view.

There is, however, too much evidence supporting it for the points raised about males and females to be dismissed (e.g. Guttentag and Bray 1976, Best 1983, Sadker and Sadker 1982, Delamont 1984c, Whyte 1985, Collard and Mansfield 1987, Weis 1989). For example, Guttentag and Bray found that, whereas girls were trying to plan their futures around more flexible sex roles, that is futures in which both parents had careers that mattered and both partners shared housework, childrearing and earning the household income, boys were not. Boys expected a future in which they did no housework, took no part in childcare, and supported a non-working wife. Lois Weis's recent study of adolescents in an American city where the steel mills had closed found the same pattern of expectations. Young women saw themselves in an egalitarian marriage, boys envisaged a traditional one.

The schools that these adolescents attended were not dealing with such issues at all. The schools did not encourage the pupils to confront their divergent expectations, or fit the girls for the labour market by equipping them with vocational skills, or train the boys in childcare and housekeeping. Instead, the schools reinforced old-fashioned sex stereotypes. They were encouraging pupils to become male and female adults fitted for a world that has vanished.

About this book

This book argues that, for a variety of reasons which are examined later, schools and other educational institutions today are enforcing a set of sex and gender roles which are more rigid than those current in the wider society. It is asserted that the sex roles demanded by educational institutions are unnecessary for the organization or the individual, and actually produce unhappiness and inequality, as well as wasting talent. The enforcement of these sex roles affects staff and pupils, yet is very rarely a conscious policy. There are taken-for-granted norms but male and female roles in schools which are hard to show in action, are even harder to eradicate. The book first shows how the everyday life of schools and classrooms is permeated with stereotyped ideas about male and female roles, and then focuses on how some schools have tried to change.

There is now a large body of literature on sex roles and education. Sophisticated arguments about the history and philosophy of education (e.g. Martin 1984) and major contributions from psychologists (e.g. Gilligan 1982) have been omitted, although the further reading chapter makes some suggestions in those fields. Also omitted is the whole area of education outside the school: further and higher education, adult education, professional and vocational education are all outside the scope of this book. Geographically, Northern Ireland is under represented, most of the examples come from Wales, Scotland and England, or from Australia and the USA. Chapters 2 and 3 of the book use data collected by a variety of researchers to show how sex and gender are routinely handled inside schools and classrooms. Chapter 2 looks at schooling for the under 12s in the nursery, infant and primary schools, and then chapter 3 examines secondary schooling. The overall perspective on classroom life adopted is elaborated elsewhere (Delamont 1983c, Stubbs 1976, 1983) and in this volume the focus is on sex and gender rather than other facets of classroom life. Chapter 4 discusses teachers – how they are trained, their staffroom life and their careers. The argument that everyday life in British schools is permeated with stereotyped ideas about male and female roles which are not explicit but are universal will have been demonstrated by the end of chapter 4. Chapter 5 deals with the many attempts to change schools which have taken place since 1970, and evaluates their effectiveness. The concluding chapter sets out some research priorities for the sociology of education, emphasizing topics we know little or nothing about, and sketches some ideas about removing unnecessary sex distinctions from the educational system.

The theoretical background

The theory underlying the book is sociological, but it is a critical, feminist sociology. That is, although the ideas of sociology and the findings of educational research are used, they are subjected to critical scrutiny where their treatment of sex differences is concerned. Central to the perspective is the distinction between sex and *gender*. These are closely linked concepts, and are frequently used in a confused and confusing way. Briefly, *sex* should properly refer to the biological aspects of male and female existence. Sex differences should therefore only be used to refer to physiology, anatomy, genetics, hormones and so forth. *Gender* should properly be used to refer to all the non-biological aspects of differences between males and females: clothes, interests, attitudes, behaviours and aptitudes, for example, which separate 'masculine' from 'feminine' life styles. Strictly speaking therefore, we should not talk of sex roles, for the roles people play in society are essentially related not to biology, but to social behaviour; that is, they should really be called gender roles. 'Sex roles' is the common usage and so was made the title of the book, but from now on 'gender' will be used to describe male versus female characteristics except where biological phenomena are being discussed.

Sex and gender are so much a part of our everyday lives from early childhood that it is almost impossible for any researcher, in biological or social sciences, to be objective or dispassionate or disinterested in the topic when he or she is studying it. In this book there will be examples of research where the fears, prejudices or unconscious assumptions of the authors will be challenged, and fresh arguments advanced from the evidence.

A few examples will show the centrality of sex and gender in our personal worlds, and in the way we use gender to classify everything about our worldview. Think about a new baby. The first question asked after 'Is it all right?' is the baby's sex. Then he or she is given a name which is almost certainly gender specific, and dressed in either pink or blue. Or take these further examples: imagine a male lecturer came into the room in a skirt; or a woman Pope; or a man applying for a job as a nanny.

Disturbing breaches of what we take for granted could be multiplied and elaborated endlessly. However, for the purposes of this book it is only necessary to argue that classifying people into *either* the male or the female category is one of our commonest activities, that it is usually done unconsciously, and challenges to our classification are disturbing. The basic polarization between male and female is usually accompanied by a deep sense of what is *natural* (i.e. correct) and what is *unnatural* (or perverted, or wrong). Appeals and references to things being natural are common, yet it is a very problematic concept. Syphilis, diphtheria and smallpox are natural. So are sour milk, cow pats, head lice and cockroaches, but we do our best to avoid or even eliminate them. Generally what happens is that 'natural' is used only to refer to things that the speaker regards as *good* – the ingredients in chocolate, motherhood, shampoo made with henbane – or as inevitable and inescapable - the aggression of males, tempests and typhoons, maternal instinct. Conversely anything that is disliked gets the label 'unnatural' attached to it whether it is found in the animal world or not. People who are scared or revolted by homosexuality often suggest it is 'unnatural' although it is found in animals and has been recorded in many different human cultures. Indeed homosexuality is certainly more natural than many contemporary pastimes such as playing the violin, water polo, ice hockey, or hang gliding.

The distinction between what is natural and what is cultural is equally hard to draw. It is especially hard to disentangle the natural, biological aspects of male and female behaviour (sex) from the cultural, adaptive ones (gender). If we wished to discover whether men are really more aggressive than women because of their biology/nature we would have to take large numbers of boys at birth and rear them as girls, and vice versa. Given the unlikelihood of this, there are widely differing opinions about the relative importance of nature and nurture, often drawn from the same pieces of research. On the whole people who have studied anthropology tend to incline towards the idea that gender is socially created, because every culture discovered across the world has such different norms for 'masculinity' and 'femininity'. War and weapon making are the only tasks which all primitive societies seem to have reserved for men while being pregnant and giving birth are universally women's work. Childrearing is *not* a women's task universally, but is often left to older children or to the elderly of both sexes.

In this book two precepts are taken for granted. First that most of the things we associate with being male or female are actually cultural although they are widely believed to be natural (i.e. biological). Secondly I believe that it is more socially optimistic, and therefore sensible, to assume that all character-istics of masculinity and femininity are cultural (i.e. part of *gender*) unless there is irrefutable evidence to the contrary. This is because biological arguments – women are naturally full of maternal instinct, blacks have generally lower IQs than whites – are usually invoked to prevent social change, social justice and equality. If we want society to improve, to be more just and egalitarian, we must assume that a substantial part of any human characteristic, be it 'masculinity' or 'intelligence', is cultural and hence open to change.

This position is adopted for two reasons, *relativity* and *feminism*. Relativity is an outlook which is frequently mis-understood. Briefly it means that the researcher believes that humans are highly plastic and adaptive, and thus a very wide range of beliefs and practices occur in different human societies. The task of the researcher is to discover what members in any particular culture or subculture believe and do, and to try to see how the beliefs and activities fit together in that society. The researcher should never dismiss ideas or actions different from her own as wrong, inferior or perverse, but should strive to grasp their role in the culture they come from. The individual person can still condemn them, but the task of the researcher is to research, not moralize. Thus the researcher who believes in cultural relativity would study apartheid beliefs among Afri-kaners to find out how they fit into Afrikaner culture, believing that extreme racism is one variety of human behaviour (e.g. Crapanzano 1985). As an individual, or as a member of a campaign like Anti Apartheid, one can condemn the beliefs as inhuman, but the researcher should still seek to understand the function and symbolic power they have in the culture from which they come. In the area of sex and gender the researcher who studies data from a variety of cultures across the world finds a very wide range of behaviours considered to be 'masculine' and 'feminine'. One culture does not allow women to milk cows because it is men's work, another does not allow men near cows because they are women's work. In one society artistic expression is a feminine sphere, in another masculine. In some places women till the fields and men sit about and look decorative, while in others this is reversed, and so on. Because the study of anthropological data shows that different societies classify different things as 'masculine' and 'feminine', the argument that most male and female behaviour is gender not sex seems to me totally convincing. Thus this book assumes that gender roles can be modified as technology, the economic system and even the education system change.

The second reason for arguing in this book that gender is more important than sex is because this is a cornerstone of feminist belief, and this is a *feminist* book. I believe there are inequalities between men and women which should be remedied so that individuals of both sexes are freer to choose their own ways of life. In particular, it will be argued that schools *reinforce*, sometimes subtly, but sometimes crudely, the wider society's ideas about gender roles, and often reinforce them in tougher form than they actually exist in the world outside. Feminists believe that women should be socially equal to men in their society: that is, all legal, financial, economic, educational and other limitations and handicaps based on sex should be removed. This book shows how pupils and teachers work in institutions where this is far from being achieved.

The data in this book

Apart from the data gathered by other researchers whose work is cited, some material used comes from published and unpublished work of my own. The first edition of the book was written while I was doing fieldwork in two English towns (Ashburton and Coalthorpe) as part of the ORACLE project (Delamont and Galton 1986). Some of that research – added to the data from the third ORACLE site (Bridgehampton) – appears in this volume. The six schools studied are called Gryll Grange, Guy Mannering, Kenilworth, Maid Marion, Waverly and Melin Court. Subsequently I have done two Welsh projects in twelve schools – one observational, one mainly using questionnaires (Upton *et al.* 1988, Pilcher *et al.* 1989a) – and spent time collecting pupils' scarey stories about school transfer in England and Wales (Delamont 1989b). Full details about those projects can be found in the cited publications. All the schools, pupils, teachers, towns and LEAs are protected by pseudonyms. Most of these data are qualitative, based on observations, interviews and pupils' writing.

2 The formative years: nursery, infant and junior school

HE PREFERS GIRLS' GAMES

Q. My grandson has always preferred girls' toys and enjoys pretend games and dressing up in high heels and long dresses. My daughter asked the doctor what to do, and he said to stop it at once. Sometimes I let him play girls' games for a while, but he cries when I stop him. What can we do?'

A. I have great sympathy with your distress, especially as the families of two of my godchildren had similar worries at one time. My goddaughter wanted to be a boy, played boys' games, only wore boys' clothes, and only had friends who were boys. Now she is an extremely feminine young woman of 20, enjoying life like any girl of this age. My godson, who is 10 and one of four brothers, has always enjoyed what might be described as girls' toys. Last Christmas he became the proud owner of a doll's house, but the other day I noticed him playing football as hard as any of the other boys. I am quite sure this situation will only become a problem if you and his mum get tense about it. I would let him go on playing with these games for reasonable amounts of time, introducing more robust stories and ideas from time to time.

This 'problem' was published on the Family page of *Woman's Realm*, on 20 June 1987, the answer coming from a 'trained family therapist'. It shows how anxious adults can be about young children who do not adhere to conventional behaviour. If the question is scrutinized, a whole range of stereotypes appear. The grandparent believes there are 'girls' toys' and 'girls' games', *and* seems to think that imaginative play ('pretend games') and dressing up are unsuitable for males. The mother seems to think the little boy has a medical problem, and the doctor apparently agreed. The expert is reassuring, but also has an idea of 'robust' stories and play behaviours which is stereotyped.

Such a letter is not unique. In 1983 the problem page of *Woman's Own* carried a similar letter, which voiced the fear unspoken in the earlier one:

Q. I hope you can advise me about my son. He's nine years old and has two younger sisters. The problem is that he's always liked playing with his sisters and their toys. I also recently found out that at breaks in school he always plays with groups of girls. On the other hand, he goes to cubs and enjoys it and when his friends call for him he'll go out to play football or ride bikes. I'm very worried that he'll grow up to be homosexual. I've told him off a few times about playing girls' games but my husband says I'm wrong to do this and he tells the boy to play with whoever he likes. He's such a good boy in other ways and very affectionate. But I can't help worrying about this problem and am much too embarrassed to ask anyone else about it.'

A. My first reaction to your problem is to say thank goodness that your husband is not one of those 'macho' fathers who want their sons to be stereotyped, aggressive he-men from the moment of birth. For he is quite right to ask you to allow the boy to grow up in his own way and have the freedom to develop all sides of his personality. It is sad that the tender, caring side is generally labelled 'feminine' and the self-assertive, active side labelled 'masculine', for this makes many people force a connection between these character-traits and the future sexual inclinations of a child. But there is absolutely no such connection. Homosexuality has far deeper roots in an individual's upbringing and environment – perhaps even in his or her personal chemistry – than the mere enjoyment of girls' company and games. So you have

absolutely no reason to worry. Your son sounds delight-
fully balanced and free to me, likely to grow into a
confident, loving adult – as long as you will let him do so
in his own way.

Over the 1980s, then, parents were expressing concern to
mass-media 'experts' about boys not behaving in sufficiently
'manly' ways. Girls who like 'male' activities seem to be less
disturbing to adults, although both sexes receive a constant
stream of messages about what appropriate behaviours are. This
chapter examines how young children are brought up, and what
their early years of school are like and how they face up to
transfer to secondary school.

The naming of children

The minute a child is given a name he or she is forced into a
classification system, which gives the baby a gender label and
tells us quite a lot of other things about the person concerned.
Thus we can tell that Ruxana and Sapanjit are probably British
of Pakistani origin; Rhian and Mair are Welsh; Bernadette and
Theresa are Catholic and probably Irish too; Ishbel and Margot
almost certainly Scots; Tracey, Stacey and Donna are working
class; while Emma, Perdita and Charlotte are middle or upper
class. All these people are also clearly female; Ibrahim, Geraint,
Joseph, Donald, Darren and Charles would be male equivalents.
Only uncommon names are ambiguous as regards gender. The
Collins Gem Dictionary of First Names (1976) has 'over 2000
names', each labelled carefully 'm' or 'f'. Only twenty-four
names are labelled 'm' or 'f'. Male and female names are also
chosen for different reasons, as this rhyme from an American
book (quoted in Walum, 1977:38-9) shows:

She's made of sunshine, sugar and spice . . . .
Someday she's bound to change her name
Now choose the one that will stay the same.

This rhyme headed a list of girls' names, while that for boys
includes the lines:

The name that polls the winning votes

The famous name that makes up quotes.

Walum argues that American parents choose pretty names for girls which are polysyllabic, 'more melodic, and softer' while boys' names are 'short, hard-hitting and explosive'. Boys' names are short in themselves, like Lance, or have short diminutives, like Josh and Nick. The names of 1,250 children at four schools in two English cities (Delamont and Galton 1986) suggest that this is true of white, English-speaking parents in Britain too. Boys' names commonly used are monosyllabic or have short abbreviations. The girls' name are polysyllabic, and fussy, pretty and pert rather than serious. The naming of children, then, labels them not only with their gender, but carries messages about strength versus frivolity. The kinds of clothes in which the children are dressed continue this gender labelling.

Clothing children

Walum (1977:42) argues that children's clothing is sharply gender differentiated:

> In a trip through an infant section of any department store . . . on the girls' racks are princess dresses, granny gowns, pink satin pantsuits, and bikinis: on the boys'. . .are baseball uniforms, tweed suits . . .astronaut pyjamas and starched white dress shirts.

The position in Britain is essentially similar. *Woman* printed this letter on 14 February 1987.

IN THE PINK
Having had four sons my only disappointment at not having a daughter was the fact that I loved the colour pink. You could put a little girl in blue, but you certainly wouldn't dream of putting a boy in pink. How things have changed! My 13 year old son is partial to pink. I've recently had to buy him a pink shirt and pink and grey jumper (and how it suits his fair hair). I've also noticed quite burly men wearing pretty pink jumpers. But I still can't find the courage to put my 20-month-old son in pink – even though I saw a gorgeous

outfit the other day. I don't think I'd even dare buy him a pink dummy in case someone said, 'Pink's for girls!' Do other readers feel pink for boys is still definitely out?'

In 1982 *Woman's Own* did a fashion spread on clothes for children under 3 featuring children of staff from the magazine. The assistant beauty editor announced that Louise (11 months) wore 'pinafores with pretty blouses and shirts' and 'all in one suits' for bedtimes which 'she makes sure are feminine in soft fabrics and pretty colours'. The home editor dressed Alice (7 months) in 'saucy outfits made up in soft colours and pretty prints'. Fashion editor Sue liked 'pretty dresses' for Katie (6 months) but agreed 'velour playsuits' were more practical. The mothers of boys – Adam (7 months) and Oliver (1 year) – used quite different vocabulary. Adam 'is a real toughie' dressed in 'rough and tumble clothes in bright colours'. Oliver's mother 'enjoys buying him "boy's" clothes' rather than the 'almost unisex things young babies wear', and he is shown in navy and white.

The Mothercare *NOW* catalogue (Summer 1989) of clothes for the 6+ age has girls in pastel jogging suits (mint, pink or lemon), while the boys' track suits are in grey, royal or navy, or display slogans about cycling (*Tour de France*, 'Race Winner') or surfing ('Ride the Waves') or are miniature baseball or American football outfits. No girl is shown dressed up as a New York Yankee or a Miami Dolphin. Boys' pyjamas are bright blue, green and red and show Disney characters, Dr Who, Rupert, monsters, or ten pin bowling. Girls' pyjamas are pastel pink, or green, or spotted with an improving motto ('Early to bed and early to rise' etc.). The baby clothes allow parents to dress children in a unisex style: navy blue and scarlet outfits are available as well as traditional pastels. A pink floral print smocked dress is available, but so too are navy and white dungarees. After the age of 4, however, the world of clothes is gender typed and so too are toys and games.

Toys and games

The toys and games bought for the British child are noticeably class biased. The affluent working-class child has different toys

bought for different purposes from the child in an 'intellec
middle-class home. The working-class child who reaches _
nursery school or day nursery may encounter the 'educational'
toys there, however, so these have a wider influence than their
sales.

Two catalogues of mass-market toys were examined, TOYS'
"R" US for Christmases 1987 and 1988, and Marshall Ward
Winter 1988. TOYS "R" US is one of the largest retailers in
contemporary Britain. In its two Christmas catalogues small
boys (all but one white) are shown with the following toys:
playing snooker (table £49.99) or table football (£19.99) twice
each, driving a battery-powered jeep (£139.99 and £299.99)
twice, doing wheelies on a BMX (£99.97) or riding a mountain
bike (£109.99), with rock guitar (£29.99), drum kit (£69.99) or
toy microphone (£19.87), and in a laser tag star helmet
(£24.89), vest (£10.97) with gun (£22.87). Little girls (all white)
are shown telephoning from toy kitchens (£64.84 and £48.87)
twice and from a Wendy house (£129.97), riding as a passenger
in a toy jeep, playing shops (£19.97), in a purple wig (£14.87),
at a toy dressing table (£29.99) and standing by her bicycle
(£84.99) admiring a boy doing wheelies on his.

There is a much wider range of male fantasy figures than
female ones. Little girls are offered the imaginary roles of Sindy
as a cafe owner or boutique owner or city girl; of Barbie as a
doctor (in 6 inch heels!) or a rock star; three varieties of fairy
princess, and Vanessa Warfield from M.A.S.K.. Boys are offered
the role models of skateboarder, Fungus the Bogeyman, the
Ghostbusters, Captain Power, Daniel and Miyaji the Karate
Kids, Defenders of the Earth, Dino-riders, Action Riders,
Thundercats, Ken as a doctor or a rock star, Mr Pablo the
Painter, Postman Pat, Knights in Armour, Brave Star fighters,
Masters of the Universe, Rambo in three disguises, Dr Terror,
Centurion Ace McCloud, a game show host and three males
from M.A.S.K.. Boys have a much richer range of characters to
play, and theirs are active and militant.

The pattern is the same when the pictures on the boxes of the
kits and games are scrutinized. Only males are shown on the
boxes of sports kits and games (Subbuteo, Superbowl, basketball,
etc.), on all but one construction kit, on all chemistry, electronics

and tool sets (on one box a girl watches a boy do the experiments!)and on the circus and farm set boxes. Girls only are shown on a painting kit and a 'keep fit' kit. Both sexes are shown on a gardening set, one construction kit, and one drawing set, plus many of the family games such as 'Pop up Pirate'.

The pictures of toys and games in the Marshall Ward catalogue occupy seventy-seven pages, and the sexual stereotyping is similar. There is only one dressing up outfit for a girl (a nurse) and a boy (Superman). Small girls are shown on the telephone while boys drive things and carry guns. There is a toy secretary's desk (£38.75) plus toy typewriter (£19.99), a toy ironing board and clothes airer (£9.99) and a model supermarket trolley and cleaners' trolley with tools (£19.99). No girl is shown using any sports kit: all the snooker tables, table football sets, skateboards and so on are being used by boys. One girl stands passively on a miniature trampoline, another carries a bag for transporting skates. No girl actually *moves* in these pages.

The minority of parents who choose toys from the Galt, Kiddicraft and Early Learning Centre (ELC) catalogues are faced with a completely different picture. ELC eschew 'tanks, guns or fashion dolls', and their catalogue is both multi-racial and non-sexist. Small girls push toy buses along make-believe roads, drive pedal cars and toy earth movers, build with construction kits, take guard at the wicket and climb on frames. Alongside the nurse uniform is a black girl in the doctor outfit, and the child cooking at the 'mini-chef kitchen centre' (£54.95) is a boy. Galt similarly shows a girl using the microscope (£5.69) and a black boy with a doll's pram (£42.38). Kiddicraft has a text written by the Newsons, and shows girl and boy babies, black and white, exploring a non-sexist world of developmental toys.

Outside these self-consciously non-sexist catalogues, males have the creative and interesting roles, females are preoccupied with keeping themselves and their surroundings clean. Feminists argue that this is restricting to boys and girls; to boys because they are not offered tender, nurturing roles or skills of cooking and cleaning while girls are not offered active or scientific roles, or any aggressive or construction activities. This not only weighs heavily on children whose interests do not 'fit' perfectly, but leads them to stereotype the other gender, as we shall see later in the chapter.

Catalogues do not tell us what toys are actually bought for children. An American study (Goodman *et al.* 1974) undertook participant observation in a large store's toy department for 30 hours in the pre-Christmas peak period. They also asked a sample of eighty-four children what presents they had received for Christmas. The observation produced several interesting conclusions. The researchers asked shoppers the age and sex of the children for whom the gifts were being bought. They found that children under 2 got very similar presents: mainly cuddly toys, and toys to develop skills in handling objects and learning shapes and colours such as blocks, rings and simple constructions. After the age of 2 sex differentiation set in. The adult buyers had rigid sex-role norms about appropriate toys *but* would make exceptions for individual children with idiosyncratic preferences. In other words, adults did not believe that a train was a suitable present for a girl but would consider buying a train for a girl who had specially asked for one. This fits the British research by John and Elizabeth Newson (1976) who reported that parents, especially mothers, were prepared to adapt to individual children's wishes. Thus a mother would take her daughter to football games, or let a boy cook, if the children wanted it, without shifting their *overall* expectations of correct behaviour for boys and girls. Given this, it seems sad that schools appear to be *less* tolerant of idiosyncrasies than parents and force children into hyper-conventional roles.

The American observers found that adult toy shoppers spent longer choosing presents for boys than for girls. The majority bought sex-differentiated toys so that, for example, no one bought a scientific toy for a girl. The toys, and the salespeople, were clearly divided to help the adults in choosing sex-differentiated toys. The women sales staff were selling the cheap toys and the simple ones, while men were selling all the most expensive items, such as bicycles and electric racing car circuits, and all the technical things such as microscopes. The researchers also found a price difference. Of toys costing under £2, 50 per cent were for girls and 31 per cent for boys, while of toys costing over $5 dollars only 18 per cent were for girls and

it for boys. This suggests an imbalance in the *price* of
ie two sexes paralleled by the researchers' findings on
presents received. They asked forty-two girls and
boys what they had been given. The two groups had
received equal numbers of presents, but whereas 73 per cent of
boys' presents were toys and games, only 57 per cent of the
girls' presents were. Girls had received far more gifts of clothes
and furniture. Rheingold and Cook (1978) examined the con-
tents of the rooms of 6 year old children, and found that girls
had dolls, passive games and arts and crafts while boys had
trucks, bricks and equipment for active sports.

This leads us to ask how families differ in their childrearing
of boys and girls. The Newsons (1976) showed that boys were
allowed more physical freedom and not kept so close to home.
This finding is replicated by Roger Hart (1979) who asked
children to describe 'the area you are allowed to play in outside
your house by yourself'. The information was plotted on maps
and checked with parents for 5 to 8 year olds and 9 to 12 year
olds. He found that the boys in both age groups had much larger
areas in which they were allowed to play, especially among the 9
to 12 year olds. In addition he found that boys changed their
environment more by building things, and that boys were more
likely to break the rules and go outside their permitted area. Not
only that, but mother knew they broke the rules and ignored the
infringement unless they got into trouble while outside the
boundary. These two pieces of research suggest parents operate
double standards between their children, with boys allowed
more physical freedom than girls.

Books and comics

Many children grow up with few books in their homes, so
discussion of books may relate more to school than home life.
There are detailed studies of the sex roles which are offered to
children in both reading schemes and 'pleasure' books reprinted
in Maccia *et al.* (1975), Stacey *et al.* (1974) and Wandor (1972).
Glenys Lobban's (1974, 1975) early findings on British reading
schemes were summarized in the first edition. During the 1970s
this concern about sexism in reading schemes reached the mass

media. In January 1978 *Good Housekeeping* ran an article asking 'Are Books Unfair to Girls?' which began:

> See John kick a football. See Jane help Mummy with the dishes. See John paddle in the water. See Jane watch from the beach. See John suggest an adventure. See Jane tag obediently along behind. See John grow into a mature person . . . See Jane, on the other hand, grow up to be a right little weed. . .

The article argued that although the best-selling series had begun to 'move with the times', there is still 'no doubt who is boss'. The books 'reflect a world that is past, or perhaps never existed', a world in which mothers do not work outside the home, and spend all their time on housework. Lobban had pointed out that boys are shown spending time watching adult men, not relatives, performing their occupational roles and tasks. Girls see only mothers. Given that mothers are never seen to have jobs (except in the *Nippers* series) girls are not shown any adult female occupational roles. Despite such research and journalism, publishers have reprinted books in the 1980s – such as Heather Amery (1983) *The First Thousand Words* – which are replete with sexism. So replete in fact that Ralph Fevre (1988) wrote to the publishers to complain and kept the book away from his daughters. Grauerholz and Pescosolido (1989) carried out a recent analysis of sex roles in children's literature from 1900 to 1984. In the early years of the century the sex ratio of child characters was equal, and became so again in the 1970s, while between 1920 and 1970 boys predominated. The sex ratio of animal characters and adults has become more and more male dominated, while the number of adult women shown, and the roles they play, are still small and restricted. *Plus ça change!*

This leads into a consideration of other texts available in infant and primary schools – elementary textbooks. Here we are dependent on American analyses, and Nilsen (1975:208) summarizes their conclusions:'

> It is ironic that in recent years, little girls lost out in two different ways. Boys are the dominant figures in the nonfiction section of the library because they are thought to be

more able than girls in such fields as maths, science, and statesmanship. Then they are the dominant figures in the beginning-to-read book for just the opposite reason. They are thought to be *less* able than girls in the fields of language arts.

So much for the reading given to children as part of their schoolwork. Most British children spend far more time with comics than books, and absorb gender stereotypes from TV, radio and advertising. The first edition summarized the analyses of comics and TV available in the 1970s. Both print and electronic media change rapidly, and analyses of sex-role messages in comics and popular TV programmes need to be done regularly. Superficially Andy Pandy and Looby Loo are very different from Thundercats, but their sex-role stereotyping is very similar.

Thus we can see that the world in which British children grow up is a gender-segregated world, in which all facets of their lives at home and in the community are deeply impregnated with stereotypes of masculinity and femininity. Boys are tough, aggressive and creative, girls mild, verbal and domestic. The Newsons (1978) suggest that children's idiosyncrasies can be tolerated inside a family, but the position changes when a child leaves home for a playgroup, day nursery or infant school. It is to these socializing and educational institutions that we now turn.

Inside schools and classrooms

At the beginning of this chapter the disquiet caused by children who tried *not* to behave in gender-stereotyped ways was discussed. To understand how most educational classes for young children are reinforcing even more rigid gender stereotypes than the wider society in which they are embedded we must examine the available data on schools and classrooms. However, although there has been a significant growth of research on interaction in schools in the last 20 years (Delamont 1983c) gender differentiation has been neglected. There are several observational studies of infant and primary education (Nash 1973, Sharp and Green 1975, Hamilton 1977) which do not discuss gender *at all*. However there is King's (1978) work on infant classrooms followed by Clarricoates (1980, 1981, 1990), Paley (1984) and Best (1983). Lindow *et al.* (1985) summarize the American research on classroom interaction, selected examples of which are collected in Wilkinson and Marrett (1985). Before examining the findings it is important to recognize that it is hard to gather data on gender divisions in an unbiased way.

Observer bias?

Clem Adelman (1979) studied pre-school classes and although his work was not intended to focus on gender differences, the fieldnotes he took show such differences and the kinds of interpretations he put on them. Adelman had a camera mounted in a robot-like structure he called Charlie. When he first took Charlie into a class the 'children were struck silent'. Then 'Sharon . . . went to Mrs S. and cuddled up to her in some sort of fright maybe, whilst at the same time a young new girl who was drinking milk with the nurse began to cry'. Quite soon though, children came forward to inspect Charlie, and then 'there were ten or twelve children, the majority of them boys, painting very vigorously the surfaces of Charlie'. Here we see two stereotyped kinds of behaviour. The little girls show fear and cry, and boys come boldly forward to try a new activity. These seem to be typical of studies of young children, but are small girls really more fearful of novelty, or is there a difference in adult interpretation of the behaviour?

We certainly have evidence that the same behaviour from a child will be interpreted differently according to the perceived and believed gender of the individual. For example, Walum (1977: 40) reports an experiment in which mothers were shown Beth, a 6 month old 'girl' in a frilly pink dress, and Adam, a 6 month old 'boy' in blue rompers. Beth was viewed as 'sweet', with a 'soft cry', offered a doll to play with and smiled at more often. In fact they were the same baby, with different 'name' and clothes. In a similar experiment film of a 6 month old baby dressed in yellow engaged in crying, crawling, smiling and so on was shown to a sample of professionals (paediatricians, psychologists, nursery nurses and so on) and amateurs (mothers and students). Half of each group of viewers were told that the baby was a boy, half that it was a girl, and all were asked to describe what the baby was doing at each stage of the film. The results were clear. All the professionals, and the students, attributed quite different motives to the same behaviour, according to the gender of the baby. If they thought it was a boy, they described it as angry when it cried; if a girl, as frightened. Only mothers did not attribute motives, but merely said that the baby was crying, crawling or whatever. Thus we do not know if Sharon was frightened of Charlie, or whether Adelman thought she was, or whether she had already learnt that adults expect girls to show fear and reward it with approval.

In part, such attribution of aggression to tiny babies according to their gender reflects a common belief that males are born 'aggressive'. Yet the evidence on this point is clearly inconclusive, and in one famous case turned out to be untenable. Many American researchers had observed new-born babies, to see if there were early signs of sex differences. Study after study showed little girl babies sleeping peacefully or lying quietly in their cots, while little boy babies yelled lustily and waved their arms and legs. The researchers concluded that from birth boys are more active and aggressive, and thus, some argued, aggression in males must be sex linked. So many different American studies showed this behaviour variation that it has ceased to be a research question, yet when some researchers in Britain attempted replication as a routine confirmation, they found that sex difference did not exist among British babies. Boys and girls in maternity hospitals did not behave in distinct ways, but slept or yelled apparently at random. This cultural difference called for some explanation, and the answer turned out to be circumcision. The American boy babies had all been circumcised at birth as a matter of routine, while British ones had not. Thus the supposed sex difference was in fact a reaction to medical treatment. All the American boy babies were in pain or discomfort, after being operated on, while the girls had not been so violated.

The main importance of these studies of perceived sex and gender differences is that they lead to differential treatment of the two categories of babies. From very early years girls are talked to and cuddled more, while boys are tossed around vigorously. Girls are seen as fragile, boys are not. From their earliest hours, boys and girls are brought up in different ways, to reinforce different behaviours, and punish or prevent 'wrong' activities. There is no real evidence on how far parents, teachers and others are conscious or unconscious of dividing and segregating the young in this way. Nor are there any data on how far educational researchers 'see' the behaviours of little boys and little girls very differently because of their preconceptions. As we read observational studies of schools and classrooms we must remember 'Beth' and 'Adam'. '

Expectations and interactions in schools

There is important evidence about teachers' expectations for boys and girls, and their performance on tests and in ordinary schoolwork, which needs summarizing here. At the infant and primary stages girls are more successful than boys in every subject except mathematics (Douglas 1964, Davie et al. 1972, Mortimore et al. 1988) and are rated more highly for good behaviour and personality by teachers. Ingelby and Cooper (1974) collected teacher ratings on 180 West Indian, Asian, Anglo-Saxon, Cypriot, and other white London primary children. Girls received more favourable ratings than boys on all the scales except sociability. Girls were seen as superior in character, brightness, schoolwork, home background and language skills. During the school year the gap between boys and girls narrowed on all the scales except schoolwork. Ethnic minority children had worse ratings than Anglo-Saxons throughout, but the gender gap was equally pronounced within each group. That is West Indian girls were rated better than West Indian boys, Cypriot girls better than Cypriot boys and so on. Hartley (1978) collected data on 393 infant-school pupils. The teacher rated the working-class pupils as untidier, noisier and less able to concentrate than middle-class pupils, and within each class, boys were rated rougher, noisier, untidier and less able to concentrate than girls. Thus girls from non-manual homes were most favourably perceived by teachers, and manual working-class boys were rated worst. Hartley also got the pupils to rate each other, and their ratings showed clear sex differences in the same direction as the teachers'. Hartley also found that the sex differences were greater in the middle class than the working class. He concludes that 'the pre-school sex-roles of children within the same social class background do not equally prepare them for the pupil role' (p.81).

Teacher ratings of children are important if they relate to teacher behaviour or are communicated to the children. There is considerable evidence that teachers' expectations for children do influence their interactions with them. Brophy and Good (1974) showed that pupils believed to be clever were given longer to answer teacher questions, and more prompts and hints to help their thinking, than pupils who were believed to be stupid. The subsequent research is summarized in Mortimore *et al.* (1988: 163–75), Good (1987) and Brophy (1985). Repeatedly, teachers are more positive about girls under 11 and have higher expectations for them. The evidence is complex on how far such expectations translate into behaviour (Bossert 1983, Lindow *et al.* 1985, Brophy 1985, Mortimore *et al.* 1988), but it does appear that boys are more often reprimanded, and given more instructions by teachers than girls.

The discussion of data on gender differentiation in schools begins with features of the formal organization. The first theme is the formal organization of the school, which may mean that pupils lead quite separate lives within the same school building. The second, third and fourth themes are all to do with teacher behaviours inside the classroom. Second is the way in which teachers can and do use rivalry and differentiation between the sexes as an integral part of their classroom management strategies. The third theme is the way in which the *teaching* may segregate and polarize boys and girls, for example by giving them academic material which is clearly labelled 'for boys' or 'for girls'. The fourth organizing theme on teacher behaviour is the ways in which teachers may differentiate between the sexes in their 'socializing', for example in conversations about pupils' clothes, hair-styles and personal possessions. The final organizing theme is the way in which *pupils* themselves may segregate the sexes, and the consequences of this voluntary segregation.

School organization and gender separation

Schools segregate the sexes in many ways. For example, lavatories, changing rooms, cloakrooms and even playgrounds may be segregated. Pupils are commonly listed separately in the register, lined up in separate groups, and offered different subjects. These organizational arrangements are so common that they are taken for granted, and hence invisible. Most researchers do not mention that schools separate even infants in this way. The school which does not divide boys from girls will, by its very oddity, reveal how normal such separations are. Carol Joffe (1971) studied a San Francisco nursery school which was self-consciously 'progressive' and wanted to eradicate racial and sexual differentiation. One strategy was to have unsegregated lavatories, and this alone was enough to upset some parents. Similarly, King (1978:67-9) claims that the official record cards in the infant schools he studied were colour coded differently for boys and girls, that all the registers listed boys and girls separately, and that 'in every classroom boys hung their coats separately from girls' and were lined up in separate rows at the door. The teachers regarded these as 'natural' and 'convenient' arrangements and thought King odd for asking about them.

Similar organizational arrangements characterized two middle schools in 'Ashburton', an English town (see Delamont and Galton 1986). In many ways Gryll Grange and Guy Mannering were as different as two schools *could* be, yet in terms of sex segregation they were identical. Both schools listed boys and girls separately on the register, so that the nurse, photographer, remedial teacher and so on called children separately by sex. Both schools had different lavatories and separate changing rooms, and both taught different games to each sex, with a master giving boys football while a woman taught girls netball. Neither school allowed girls to wear trousers. Lining up by sex before and after any activity meant the children sat apart, because the boys had led and the girls followed or vice versa.

Best's (1983) description of life at Pine Hill, an American elementary school, makes exactly the same points. In these ways the children were constantly reminded that they were either male or female even when this was irrelevant to the activity in which they were engaged. This organizational segregation would not, in itself, be significant if it were not just the first of many ways in which school life separates and then stereotypes boys and girls. School organization is reinforced by classroom management to which we now turn.

Classroom management

Teachers in many nursery, infant and junior schools regularly use sex and gender as an organizing principle and a management strategy within their classrooms. King (1978:52) offers some fine examples such as the teacher saying, 'Boys close eyes. Girls creep out, quietly get your coats. Don't let the boys hear you!'. This shows a teacher using sex segregation to motivate and to control children, a combination which is extremely common. Later King quotes a mistress ridiculing a child with the comment 'Oh, Philip is a little girl. He's in the wrong queue' (p.68) as a disciplinary strategy. This is a common teacher usage. King also noted a class where, when acting Humpty Dumpty, 'Mrs Pink makes the girls horses and the boys King's men' (p. 68). Lubeck (1985:130) reports similar strategies from a Head Start pre-school, such as the teacher organizing pupils before lunch:

> Boys, get on your yellow line. Now girls. . . . Now when you go inside the toilets, no wrassling, boys, I'm coming too.

Clarricoates (1987: 199) watched when:

> A male teacher informed a games class in Dock Side, who were clambering over items of sports apparatus, that the girls were 'beating' the boys in climbing up the rope. Almost immediately the boys went into a paroxysm of activity in order to prove that they were 'better'.

Vivian Paley (1984: 60–2) an experienced elementary teacher in Chicago, reports herself dividing kindergarten children by sex. The school was having a Chinese New Year parade, and the class wanted to make a large dragon. Paley decides, for control purposes, that two smaller dragons would be better, and so:

> The boys and girls are to walk in adjacent rows, holding the two dragons . . . boys on the right, girls on the left.

The boys' dragon gets badly torn as they fight underneath it, and Paley regrets she did not choose mixed teams to carry them. Exactly similar patterns were found in Gryll Grange and Guy Mannering among 9 year olds. For example, at Gryll Grange the pupils had to complete a worksheet which asked them to measure features of the room such as the length of the window sills, the height of the doors and so on. Throughout one morning the teacher encouraged the class to hurry and complete this work, and her incentive was a race between boys and girls:

> Miss Tweed announces, 'I'm still waiting for most of the boys to do that measuring . . .'. (Later) Yvette has finished measuring her worksheet. Miss Tweed says, 'Another girl finished'. . . .(Later when Tammy and Stephanie are up) Miss Tweed says, 'Only seven girls to go'. Someone asks how many boys and the answer is lots . . . . Later when Kenneth is up for marking Miss Tweed says, 'Only five girls to go now'. 'How many boys?' 'Nearly all of them.'

This was Gryll Grange, a 'progressive' school, but Guy Mannering was equally characterized by gender-typing. For example, in a cookery lesson the home economics teacher said:

> *Boys* – is it boys who are making so much noise or is it a group of girls? . . . . Be careful boys that you get your tables all nice and straight.

Incidentally, cookery may nowadays be done by both boys and girls, but as King (1978:43) also shows, they are clearly distinguished in the school kitchen. He quotes:

> Teacher: What must you do before any cooking?
> Children: Roll up your sleeves and wash your hands.
> Teacher: Right, girls go first.

The boys put on green-striped aprons and girls flowery ones. A number of further incidents will show how typical sex separation is in discipline, motivation and control.

> Communal singing in the Hall. Two teachers and all six first year classes (180 pupils). Towards the end of the lesson they sing *There's a Hole in My Bucket* with the sexes divided. Boys are told to 'pretend to be a bit gormless. I know you're not'. (*Guy Mannering*)

> (In Maths) There is a wasp in the room. Mrs Forrest asks a boy to get rid of it. He kills it.(*Guy Mannering*)

> Music with Mr Vaughan. Has pupils clapping rhythms – has two girls doing it alone, then two boys. After playing part of *Peter and the Wolf* has scale singing – competing boys versus girls. (*Gryll Grange*)

> Miss Tweed's class are going to have their school photographs taken. The girls are sent first. (The photographer is in the foyer with a blue backcloth hung up). . . . Kenneth has made 82 + 47 equal over 300. Held up for public ridicule, told he should be the Chancellor of the Exchequer and that 'Scotsmen don't usually make mistakes over money'. Girls are told 'You've done enough fussing. I know you're all filmstars' and asked about the photographer, 'Did he faint with delight at such loveliness?'. (*Gryll Grange*)

This last extract shows the use of gender labelling in discipline, where boys are shamed by reference to adult males in responsible positions, while girls are exhorted to be beautiful. These kinds of controlling strategies shade into teaching, where gender roles are again clearly separated as the next section will show.

Teaching

Teachers in nursery, infant and primary schools value instruction both in basic skills and in social and emotional development (Ashton *et al.* 1975, Ashton 1981). In both kinds of instruction they are, on the evidence available, polarizing and differentiating boys and girls and reinforcing quite different behaviour patterns. Lisa Serbin (1978) spent 5 years observing fifteen pre-school classrooms in New York working in four schools. She offers the following account of the build-up to Easter in 1971 as a typical example of teacher instruction in social behaviour. The teacher played *Here Comes Peter Cottontail* while the boys hopped all over the room. Then the girls had a turn as rabbits. Next the teacher played *In Your Easter Bonnet* while the girls paraded. The teacher said, solemnly:

> Ladies, that isn't the way we have a parade. When we have a parade, we all walk very nicely, and we pick up our feet so we don't make lots of noise on the floor, and we all walk like little ladies. Now let's do it again.

She played again and the girls tiptoed. A boy asked for a second turn for boys. So the teacher played *Here Comes Peter Cottontail* again. No one said the boys should be quiet.

Serbin's observations show a typical incident with young schoolchildren, where the teaching is about social behaviour as much as any intellectual content, and the social behaviour is highly stereotyped. Other observations Serbin made were that boys got a great deal more teacher attention than girls whether they were physically close to the teacher or not, while girls only got attention when they were physically close to the teacher. The staff told Serbin that little girls were boring, and clung too closely to them, while boys were more independent. These teachers did not realize that their own interaction patterns were reinforcing the very behaviour they disliked. Little *girls* had to stay close behind the teacher to get any attention, while boys did not. The kind of teacher–pupil interaction was also different for boys and girls. Boys got more teacher interaction, more ticking off, more praise, and a different type of instruction. Boys got 'more detailed step-by-step instruction in how to solve a problem or how to do something for themselves'. Serbin found that boys got eight times as much instruction as girls, and when teachers were faced with this, they said that girls picked up things by themselves, while boys needed teaching.

Serbin also looked at what children chose to play with, and found that those pre-school children who played with bricks, trucks and climbing apparatus were better at all the problem-solving tasks involving visual spatial reasoning. In contrast children who played with dolls and housekeeping materials were better at fine motor tasks. Among these children the two sets of abilities were not totally sex specific, although it was predominantly boys who played with the bricks, trucks and climbing apparatus, and primarily girls who played at housekeeping tasks. Serbin found that teachers were reinforcing the incipient sex segregation. When there were three new toys in the classes, a fishing game, a sewing game and a counting puzzle, the staff told the classes that they could go fishing like Daddy and sewing like Mommy. Then they got boys to demonstrate the fishing game and girls to demonstrate the sewing game. Serbin was also aware that the staff had a biased pattern of object usage. They spent their time among the 'teaching tasks' and did not go over to the bricks and trucks. This meant that girls, who stayed close to the teachers, never went near the bricks or cars. The researchers then asked the teachers to go to the area where the bricks were, and when they did, the girls went with them and began playing with bricks and cars. Similarly, teachers spent little time with dolls, but if a teacher did go and work with them, boys would follow her there. Serbin says, 'In about ten minutes the whole block corner was occupied by boys and girls, half the children had never been in that area before'. In other words if the teacher encouraged girls to play with 'male' toys by going to work with them herself, girls would play with them, and girls who did improved their spatial reasoning. Yet before the researchers showed the teachers how they were failing to get all children involved in all kinds of task, teachers were unaware of it. If Serbin's observations are true in Britain (and the work of Adelman (1979) suggests they might be) then some action research to encourage each gender to develop all its skills by trying all toys and games seems a priority.

King's (1978) work on infant schools shows how instruction in social skills and academic matters are closely tied together. For example:

(A boy has found a snail in the wet sand box)
When a girl went to touch it, the teacher said, 'Ug, don't

touch it, it's all slimy. One of the boys, pick it up and put it outside' (p.43).

Just the thing to encourage scientific curiosity. Peterson and Fennema (1987) found one elementary school teacher who taught her class about a famous man who had been born in each month of the school year. At the end of the year a parade for parents consisted of twelve boys playing these twelve great Americans. The girls carried placards with the name of the month and the man. Best (1983:60) found that at Pine Hill:

> In Kindergarten the teacher encouraged girls to play in the doll house, but no boy ever played there. Wheeled toys and building equipment like Lego blocks and erector sets were routinely assigned to boys but not to girls .... When I suggested to the principal that the boys might like to play in the doll house . . . he agreed but said, 'If I encourage boys to play in the doll house, the community will run me out'.

Lubeck (1985:106) noted that in the Head Start kindergarten:

> For Thanksgiving children were shown how to paste Indian feathers, previously cut out by the aide, onto a construction paper band. All of the girls had three feathers: all of the boys had one each.

A similar pattern was common in the lessons for 9 year olds at Gryll Grange, as the following extracts show:

> In Mrs Hind's class, pupils are writing their own sentences, each one including three words from the board. The word trios are:
> boy football window
> gorilla cage keeper
> monkeys coconuts hunters
> soldier army tank
> Several ask her about the words so she reads through them. Says of 'soldier army tank'
> 'That's one for the boys really I suppose'.

Here we see an entirely gratuitous comment by a teacher implying only boys are interested in warfare. It adds nothing to the lesson, and indeed detracts from it. (It might be good to offer pupils less stereotyped sets of words such as 'girl football window' 'WRAC army tank', just to see what pupils did.)

> French with Miss Tweed. Miss Tweed can get lots of pupil involvement in French by saying '*C'est une fille*' and pointing to a boy, and vice versa. . . . When we get on to individual children answering one girl says she doesn't know whether Ralph is a girl or a boy. Miss Tweed makes a great joke about it, 'been here a week and a half and you don't know if "it" is a boy or a girl'.
>
> Sammy can reduce the whole class to laughter by pointing to Kenneth and saying *Voila Maman*. Nanette can do the same thing, and joke does not pall. . . . Duncan calls Malcolm a girl which is very funny to class.
>
> Go back to tape. Miss Tweed divides them into boys and girls, the boys are to copy the man on the tape, the girls are to copy the woman.
>
> 11.24 *P.E* as Mr Valentine appears to take the boys to football, Miss Tweed says *C'est Maman* and gets laughter.

French, a language with gender-differentiated words, is a new idea to the pupils. Teaching the crucial difference between *une fille* and *un fils* using the pupils' sense of humour may be good instructional technique. However, it reinforces the idea that males and females are completely different, and any confusion is a source of hilarity. Sometimes there is not even an instructional strategy. Mr LeGard at Guy Mannering managed to put sex stereotyping into a library lesson on 'The Book'

> He tells them on the title page there will be the author's name, and that tells you something about the book. You may recognize the author and therefore know he is a good one. 'If you get a chemistry book by a senior master at a big school he ought to know what he is talking about but if it is by someone who is just a housewife, *well*!'.

Clearly the housewife must stick to her real job, and not branch out.

At Kenilworth, in a music lesson Mr Tippett was introducing the stringed instruments

> Mr Tippett gave out a large number of broken and derelict violins. He said they were not all complete but they would do for drawing. . . . He began by saying that violins were like young ladies: they are fairly big at the top, they are small-waisted, and they have got . . . err 'Big bums' says a child.

> 'Yes, that is right, large bottoms' says Mr Tippett.
> Then he asked what the *family* the violin belonged to was called. Luella said 'The strings'.

> In Mrs Hind's class. Boy is up at her desk. She reads aloud from book 'Mary says she likes looking after people who are ill. What would she like to be when she grows up?'. The answer is, of course, 'a nurse'. Doctor is not mentioned as a possible answer. . . . Mrs Hind tells Kenton to show his book to Janice to help her draw an aeroplane. (*Gryll Grange*)

Here we see a highly stereotyped piece of teaching material, an English comprehension book. Women are nurses, not doctors. It is also noticeable that the teacher does not add the idea of a woman being a doctor to counteract the sexism of the book, which she could easily do. We also see an example of one pupil being asked to teach another, which is a feature of a 'progressive' school. However, the particular example shows an assumed male superiority in the sphere of machinery/transport. The girl is not told to find out about aeroplanes, but to ask a male.

> In Miss Tweed's class for a Maths test. There are mixed questions, straight calculations and problems such as 'If you were sent by your mother to buy half a dozen eggs, how many would you bring her?'.

This is again an example of unnecessary sex typing in academic materials. Why say it is 'mother' who sends for food and is responsible for providing meals? It could just as easily be 'Dad' sending for the eggs, but it is not. Teaching materials are full of such implicit sexism, which are never counterbalanced by maths problems about Dad going shopping, or Mum digging a trench. If teaching materials and interaction about academic matters is peppered with such stereotyping, then the 'social' interaction between teachers and pupils is smothered in them as the next section shows.

Socializing

Carol Joffe (1974) studied a San Francisco nursery school, and concluded that girls' clothes and appearance were far more frequently complimented than boys', *and* that girls got more compliments when wearing dresses than trousers. Boys were much more likely to be admired for fighting: teachers would make comments such as 'he really can take care of himself like a man'. Yet the nursery staff were trying to encourage *non-sexist* behaviour. Most schools have no such aim, and data from Ashburton and Bridgehampton show essentially similar patterns of social interaction to those found by Adelman among pre-school children.

Some of the comments recorded in classrooms, such as Mr Tippett's joke about violins, are pure sexism. For example when Mr LeGard taught 1.5 at Guy Mannering about 'the timetable'

> He hands them out some red books and says that they are going to do an exercise on timetables which 'are always regarded as being complicated, but they are not once you find your way around'. A page has a timetable for a bus route from Eastbourne to Hastings. 'We have the page from the bus timetable, the first information you get is the number of the bus. That's useful. Then it tells you where it goes from Eastbourne, Pevensey, Bexhill, and Hastings. That's general, now we get to the timetable itself.'

Mr LeGard then explained how to read a bus timetable, and the children were left to work through a series of questions on this timetable. After 10 minutes, Mr LeGard read out the answers for the pupils to mark their own. All the boys reported getting at least seven out of ten correct; some girls reported only getting two, three or four correct, while Mair and Leila got all ten right and a credit. Mr LeGard, however, discounts their achievements:

Apart from Mair and Leila, the old thing has come up again, that a man can use a timetable better than a woman.

Pupils' views

Of course it would be ridiculous to suggest that teachers are enforcing sex differentiation upon pupils to whom it is unknown. Pupils come to school with clearly stereotyped ideas about boys and girls. Guttentag and Bray (1976: 284) found that among 10 year olds each sex stereotyped the other. Boys thought girls were neat, sensitive, gentle, cautious, good looking, obedient, quiet, apt to cry a lot, and weak! The children actually operated a triple standard. Both sexes were committed to the idea that they could try anything as individuals, that their same-sex peers could break the rules of masculinity and femininity to some extent, but that children of the opposite sex must be rigidly conventional. So it was, in David's eyes, fine for him to be a ballet dancer, but not really suitable for his mates, and unthinkable for Karen to be an airline pilot.

Best (1983) and Clarricoates (1987) have many examples of children's stereotypes impinging on their peers. Clarricoates (1987) was told about Michael:

When Miss Mackeson asked him what he wanted to be when he grew up he said he wanted to be a butterfly. He's just a great big sissy. (p.191)

Minns (1985) transcribed a taped discussion of pupils' responses to *Charlotte's Web*, during which children 'explained' why girls cried:

Clayton: Only the boys didn't cry 'cos they were brill. . . . We don't cry like girls. They're babies.
Karen: Miss, I think why the boys didn't cry is because the girls are more sensitive than boys at stories like that.
Tracy: I think I know why girls sometimes cry, 'cos they take things more serious than boys do.
Clayton: . . . Men don't cry when spiders die. Women do, they're so stupid.

Best's (1983) book is called *We've All Got Scars*, because the 8 year old boys at Pine Hill told her scars marked a proper male. Jonathan told Best that to be in a high status boys' clique scars were a prerequisite, because they showed the boy had fought and climbed and fallen.

Children not only hold stereotyped views about the opposite sex, they also segregate themselves. Joffe (1971) saw three girls who had climbed on top of a large structure in the playground. A (male) comes over and C screams, 'Girls only!' to which A screams back, 'No, boys only!'. Similar incidents are reported in Sussman (1977), Clarricoates (1987) and Paley (1984). Karkau (1976) found that boys and girls of 9 rarely mixed: forming separate groups, playing different games and rarely talking to each other. His pupils even had a taboo on touching or approaching a person of the opposite sex. Girls told him that if they went near boys 'People will think you're "in love" ', and boys said 'If you touch a girl you get "cooties" or "girl-touch" ' which Karkau describes as 'a mysterious quality which can only be removed by saying "no gives" '. When Karkau asked his class about segregation in the playground the boys said that girls *could* play soccer with them, but the girls pointed out that the boys never asked, only boys were captains of teams, the boys did not pass the ball to girls, and if a girl scored, the boys did not cheer. The boys agreed that all these criticisms were true. Similar observations are recorded in Best (1983) and Clarricoates (1987).

Rivalry between boys and girls is revealed in the following incidents:

> This morning there was obvious sex rivalry in racing to get changed after swimming – as pupils were waiting in the foyer for their classmates to emerge from the changing rooms so they could all come back to school there were occasional whispers from the girls: 'Three boys and four girls, we're winning. Oh now we're not' as more boys emerge from their changing room. (*Gryll Grange*)

> They do competitive counting. All stand up and say numbers in French in turn. If wrong they sit down. Davina is the last one on her feet. When Maurice was the only boy left there

were mutters from other boys that he should win for the boys. (*Gryll Grange*)

English with Mr Evans. Pupils can have one book between two. Dominico and another boy are given the books to distribute. Told to give one between two and then give out spares, Dominico and the other boy give out one between two, and Mr Evans says that they must not give all the spare copies to the boys, but must be 'democratic' – he finds a girl for the last spare copy. (*Guy Mannering*)

One consequence of the pupils' views and behaviour is that when mixed groups were formed, the task did not get done, as in the following extract from notes on a PE lesson at Guy Mannering:

Pupils are told to get into threes. Girls organize themselves but boys don't. Teacher puts Terence with Coral and Lauretta to the giggles of other boys. The threes are told to get a bench and place it in a specific locality (to do exercises on).

Terence, Coral and Lauretta did not co-operate well; no PE was done by that trio. There is evidence that the more 'progressive' the class, the more polarization there is. Sussman (1977) studied 'progressive' elementary schools in the USA to investigate the hypothesis that where there is 'partial withdrawal of the teacher's authority' (p.xiii) the vacuum is filled by peer group authority. After observation in a variety of schools she found that:

(In a black ghetto school first grade class)
The children's groupings in the room seemed during observation to be quite fluid. . . . The only line of segregation was between the sexes. Ironically, when children are left to group themselves, there is more sex segregation than in teacher-made groups. (p.138)

(In the second grade class of the same school)
In this classroom, there was a fairly clear-cut division of peer groups, not only by sex, but by ethnicity and ability as well. (p.148)

Sussman studied an upper-class school where the 'underground' life pre-occupied the pupils and

> There was a intensive struggle for control of a 'fort' which the boys had built on the playground. They would not let 'outsiders' in. Outsiders included all girls. . . . Girls who tried to gain entry on one day were physically attacked by the boys, knocked to the ground, and had their coats torn off. (p. 178)

> (In the fifth and sixth grade)
> We remarked that it was interesting, for instance, that when she gave her pupils a chance to change their seats at tables all the shifts were in the directions of segregating girls and boys more completely. (p.193)

Sussman found this sex polarization disturbing, and makes it one major indictment of 'progressive' classrooms. Readers may argue that if pupils separate themselves in this way, it is because such divergence is 'natural' and schools should accept it. All kinds of things may be done 'naturally' by the pupils which schools will not tolerate for a moment, and such segregation should be one of them. After all no school would allow pupils to build a fort for 'black children only', 'council house children only', 'Catholics only', or 'Band A children only'. Any school which heard those cries would attempt to democratize the fort. Yet children are allowed to be sexist even in 'progressive' schools. Clarricoates (1987) has shown in her comparative study of four infant schools with intakes from different social classes that gender divisions are manifested in contrasting ways.

Data from the ORACLE project (Tann 1981) give an academic reason for worrying about pupils' own hostilities. Systematic observation shows that when mixed groups of pupils are required to co-operate upon tasks in the classroom they do not. Teachers who want boys and girls to co-operate on tasks must, therefore, struggle to overcome pupils' sex segregation and hostility.

Thus far the chapter has focused on children in the stereotypically 'feminine' atmosphere of primary schools. At 10 or 11 or 12 or 13 a school transfer looms, when pupils have to move to a more impersonal and more sexist environment where men must be men.

Through the postern of fate

In Flecker's poem the *Gates of Damascus*, the four gates of the city are each given a specific character. The West Gate leads to Lebanon and the sea, the North Gate is the route to Aleppo, and the South to Mecca. Travellers are able to pass through these in relative serenity. The East Gate, guarding the road to Bagdad (*sic*), is a different matter. To the east lies the desert, and nameless terrors, and probable death. Travellers are urged 'Pass not beneath', and the gate is labelled: Postern of Fate, the Desert Gate, Disaster's Cavern, Fort of Fear.

Pupils preparing to transfer from junior schools to secondary ones face that *status passage* with similar apprehension. (Status passage is the social science term for the period when we move from one status to another. Being engaged is the status passage from being single to being married for example.) What is clear from all the studies of pre-transfer anxieties is that issues of gender are one important strand within them. Pre-adolescent and adolescent boys believe that they are moving to an institution where their credentials *as males* will be inspected and their masculinity tested. This is clear from two sensitive American books (Best 1983, Fine 1987) and from all the British work on transfer anxiety. The commonly told 'scare stories', urban legends (Brunvand 1983), myths (Morin 1971) or rumours (Shibutani 1966) about what awaits pupils beyond their postern of fate carry some awful warnings about what happens to small, new pupils at secondary school.
The common myths are:

  the lavatory, shower, rubbish bin myth
  the laboratory rat myth
  the 5 mile run myth
  the violent gang myth
  the weird/strict teacher myth
  the supernatural phenomena

An example of each is given below, taken from data collected either during the ORACLE project (Delamont and Galton

1986) or by Measor and Woods (1984) or by Delamont during 1987–9 in Wales or in 'Ledshire.'

Lavatory myth   Before I went to Rowberry Common High School I was told by my sister that when the older pupils found out it was my birthday they would flush my head down the toilet.

Rat myth   Two stories my sisters told me before I went to the Grammar School they had both attended. Both stories turned out to be true though I didn't believe them at the time. 1. cutting up rats and human eyes for Biology. . . .

The cross country run myth   Measor and Woods (1984: 21–2) say:

Many boys repeated with some alarm the view that, at the new school, you were frequently expected to go on long distance runs, especially if there was (*sic*) snow on the ground. Mark said, 'And they say you have to run to Brookfield and back'. And Bruce, 'some kids told me, in PE you run to Brookfield and back – it's nearly five miles!'.

Violent gangs   Before I went to Poynings school I was told by friends that there was an older boy who had been in trouble with the police for GBH (Grievous Bodily Harm) using a chain with spikes on and the rest of the fifth years were to be scared of.

The weird teacher myth   Before I went to Westhaven High School I was told by my sister that there was a history master who hung people from the light fittings by their toenails if they didn't do their homework.

The supernatural phenomena   Before I went to the senior school at the Ledchester Convent I was told by older pupils that the corridors by the chapel were haunted by the 'white lady'. Once some boarders had ventured down one night and had seen this apparition. The nun had lunged at one of the girls, missed, and hit the wall where the imprints of her fingernails can still be seen.

These have been discussed in more detail elsewhere (Bryan 1980, Measor and Woods 1983, 1984, Delamont and Galton 1986, 1987, Delamont 1989b). Here the gender implications of these rumours is the focus. As Measor and Woods pointed out, these myths suggest that secondary schools are places where there will be:

New demands of harshness and toughness. . . . in both formal and informal cultures. (p. 19)

For Measor and Woods:

The secondary school represents a new, more impersonal state, where the inner self cannot any longer be safely revealed. (p.20)

Boys have to face up to these new demands, or they will be branded as poofters – like the boy KK whose letter to the *TV Times* was quoted at the beginning of the book. Male pupils have to claim that they are looking forward to dissecting the rat, doing that 5 mile run, and so on. They have to be prepared to face up to the bullies in the lavatories and playground and to the most weird and fearsome types of teacher including the gay master, such as this one from Ledshire:

That the art teacher was gay and put favourite boys in his dark room.

The informal culture of pupils circulates these stories, which carry clear messages about what proper male and female secondary pupils do. To the adult outsider, primary schools may look sexist. To pre-adolescents, the approaching secondary school is the place where sex roles will become critical. The next chapter looks at what happens in secondary school.

3 The adolescent in school

'A friend wants to come over to do some recording on my cassette player,' said my teenage son. 'Tim's into heavy metal.' Oh dear, I thought what am I letting myself in for? Well, the music which boomed out wasn't my cup of tea but when I walked into the room, there was no wild, headbanging orgy taking place, just a quiet young lad sitting on the settee doing embroidery! Not a traycloth nor a cushion cover, I hasten to add, but a denim jacket with an intricate design of a pop group's logo. I learned later that he is doing three A-levels, including higher maths and physics. Perhaps our teenagers are not the stereotypes we often think them and I, for one will try to look beyond the labels in future.

This was the Star Letter in *Woman* on 16 January 1988. Again the pressures of the conventional view of appropriate male and female behaviour are apparent. Why a young man interested in heavy metal should not embroider a traycloth if he wished to is not specified, but it is clear that designing stage clothes for a rock group is permissible where cushion covers would not be. This chapter examines how schools respond to adolescents and adolescents to schools. It begins with a discussion of social science research on adolescence, and then secondary school processes are examined. The pupils whose fears about secondary education ended Chapter 2 are entering not only a new type of school, but also a new stage of their lifecycle.

The adolescent society?

There is a very large literature on adolescence from which it is clear that many adult social scientists are extremely anxious about people between 12 and 21. The majority of authors project their anxieties and doubts on to adolescents, and there are dozens of books which stress how confused, disturbed, easily led astray and vulnerable adolescents are. There is not, however, very much research on how adolescents see their own lives, not much sociology, and the literature has some very clear biases and omissions. Adolescents are researched if they are deviant or delinquent, and not if they are normal or conformist. Adolescent boys are researched if they are working class but not otherwise. Adolescent girls are researched if they are promiscuous or pregnant, but not otherwise. Hell's Angels are studied but not Boy Scouts; Children of God but not members of the Methodist Youth Club and so on. Researchers on adolescence have been tempted by the bizarre and exciting, not the respectable and conventional.

Researchers and commentators have generally been extremely ambivalent about young people. In their introduction to *Working Class Youth Culture*, Mungham and Pearson (1976:1) pointed out that adolescents were portrayed either as 'rebellious, ill-fitting members of a well-ordered world; or glorified as potential rebels . . . who will overturn a world which is sick, lifeless and dull'. Attempting to bring some order to the confused debate, Mungham and Pearson emphasized the sloppiness of most writing about young people, which talks loosely of 'generation gaps' and 'problems'. They prefered to see 'youth culture', not as a unitary phenomenon, but as something differentiated by class, occupation, education, ethnic identity and sex. In this they shared the opinion of most of the level-headed commentators on adolescence. However, their own collection and the volume from Hall and Jefferson (1975) which appeared at about the same time both perpetuated one of the worst flaws in the literature on adolescents: its neglect of gender divisions. Mungham and Pearson claimed (1976:4) that they could not find anyone to write about the lives of working-class adolescent girls; while Hall and Jefferson included one theoretical note and a short article which drew on data collected in a youth club.

Those two collections date from the early 1970s. Since then there have been some studies of young women (e.g. McRobbie 1990, Smith 1978, Wilson 1978, Lees 1986, Coffield *et al.* 1986,

Wallace 1987) and of female school pupils (notably Griffin 1985 and Davies 1984). However, it is noticeable that much of the work on females appears only in scattered articles rather than books (see Delamont (1989d: 273) for the details of this). It is also striking that many authors ignore gender despite the existence of recent research on females. Marsland (1983) has written a review of the literature on 'youth' which deals only with men. Only research on males is reviewed, only male authors cited, yet Marsland never explains his focus.

The lack of attention to gender distinctions in the research on adolescence is one of the major flaws in it. Apart from the attention paid to deviant or delinquent youth the methods used in nearly all the studies are biased by the conscious or unconscious preconceptions of their devisors. Detailed attention to nearly every study published reveals such in-built sexism in the methods. For example, Irene Jones (1974) scrutinized *Mass Media and the Secondary School* by Murdock and Phelps (1973), and raised considerable doubts about their conclusions. One particular aspect of the research struck Jones because of its implicit assumptions. The researchers offered a sample of 322 girls and 299 boys a series of teenage role models with which to identify themselves or not as they chose. Some of these role models were common to both sexes, but some were only offered to either the boys or the girls.

Jones argues that by offering certain roles only to one sex and not the other, Murdock and Phelps were creating polarized results and forcing the two sexes into different, stereotyped roles, rather than undertaking a study without preconceptions. The roles offered to both sexes were good pupil, rebel, ritualist, good bloke/good friend, and pop fan. Boys were also offered street peer, sports fan, boyfriend, and natural leader; while girls were given homemaker, tomboy, girlfriend, and fashion follower. While the girlfriend/boyfriend pairs were matched, the other roles offered only to one sex or the other reinforce crude stereotyping. There is no role of natural leader in the girls' list nor any equivalent of it. Thus no data are available on what proportion of girls saw themselves as leaders. Equally stereotyped is the existence of roles as homemaker and fashion follower for girls (while denying them the option of street peer or sports fan) yet not offering boys any home-centred role (model builder, carpenter, etc.) or any interest in fashion and clothes. Effectively, therefore, Murdock and Phelps pre-ordained that girls would come out home centred and sheep-like, boys street centred and aggressive. Much research on teenagers has suffered from having preconceptions built into it, and has to be read with scepticism.

There is one finding from the literature on adolescence that is particularly important for schooling: the role of the peer group as a source of influence on young people. Young people derive many of their values from their homes, but as they move into adolescence their friends' ideas on music, fashion, sexuality and schoolteachers become increasingly important. When pupils face transfer to secondary school, they fear the loss of friends made in the lower school and an absence of friendship in the new one. Peer groups, or cliques, are a major factor in adolescents' school lives.

Peer groups and pressures

The importance of friendship groups among boys in school has certainly been widely documented (e.g. Hargreaves 1967, Lacey 1970, Willis 1977, Beynon 1985a). Membership of, and adherence to the norms and values of, a particular peer group can make a difference to the school attainment and involvement of boys. A boy whose friends work hard and share the teachers' values is likely to work hard and be tuned in to the teachers' values himself. He and his friends are likely to dress in clothes the school approves of, be ambitious for academic success, and enjoy different kinds of leisure activity and pop music from other groups. In contrast, groups like Willis's 'lads' will avoid schoolwork, reject teachers' standards, dress in unapproved styles, do not want academic success, and choose other kinds of leisure. And, as Hargreaves (1967) and others have pointed out, adherence to peer group norms, if they are anti-school, will be stronger than any pressure the school can exert.

Much of this research focused on anti-school or deviant pupils. More recently Aggleton and Whitty (1985) have discussed middle-class adolescents and John Abraham (1989a, b) has produced an account of two different anti-school groups in the late 1980s – one the same type of rebel as Hargreaves's from the 1960s and Willis's from the 1970s, the other (gothic punks) very different in style and philosophy. The gothic punks were disliked by some staff for having female friends, disliking football, and enjoying art – in short for being 'effeminate'.

Whether peer groups have functioned in the same ways among girls over the past 30 years is not known. Furlong (1976, 1984) argued that the whole idea of a group was too static, and analysed the classroom behaviour of West Indian girls in London via the more fluid notion of the *interaction set*, which changed from one context to another. However, Lambart (1977, 1980), Meyenn (1980), Llewellyn, Fuller (1980) and Delamont (1976b, 1984a, b) all found girls' peer groups in schools during the 1960s and 1970s which did function as important parts of their members' lives and did mediate school experience through group attitudes.

Meyenn (1980) found that the 12 and 13 year old girls in an English middle school did have groups of friends rather than one best friend, and their groups were important to them. One girl, Diane, is quoted as saying 'if we had to say somebody who was our best friend you wouldn't say one person. It would be all this lot'. Meyenn found that the sixteen girls were in four groups, which he called 'P.E.', 'nice', 'quiet', and 'science lab.'. The quiet girls saw themselves as 'dunces' and were in bottom groups for lessons. Yet they were not anti-school, but accepted their low status and co-operated to have fun. The 'nice' girls were apparently concerned to go through school unnoticed, neither excelling nor failing. The two more visible groups were the 'P.E.' and 'science lab.' girls. Both these groups wore fashionable clothes and make up, but differed in the relationship to the school. The P.E. girls were noisy and aggressive, and helped each other with schoolwork. The science lab. girls were regarded by the teachers as mature and had internalized the idea that schoolwork was competitive and individual. Their 'maturity' meant they were allotted the task of caring for the animals in the science lab. and recognized the value of their privilege. The science lab. and P.E. girls did not get on very well together, for as Diane (a science lab. girl) says 'When we get good marks they all say "teacher's pet" and things like that' while a P.E. girl,

Betty, told Meyenn about the science lab. group 'They're always trying to get round the teachers and everything. They're always teachers' pets, them four.'

Meyenn found that none of these girls was a real discipline problem for the staff, because even anti-school cliques of girls are not, apparently, actively disruptive or aggressive to teachers as boys are. Hargreaves *et al.* (1975:31) in a study of school deviance actually say that 'teachers very rarely talked to us about "difficult" girls'. Meyenn's data are very similar to Ball's (1981) from Sussex and mine on upper-middle-class 14 year olds collected in Scotland (Delamont 1984a, 1989d). At St Luke's there were similar distinctions between girls who had adopted fashion and make up and those who had not, and between those who accepted the school's ideas about intellectual effort against those who saw schoolwork as a task to be completed by fair means or foul (e.g. copying). Data are needed on far more girls in many more kinds of schools from all over Britain to establish if girls too have strong peer groups which function to mediate between the individual and the school. (Better data on boys would also be useful and illuminating!)

Another aspect of adolescent life has frequently been uncovered by researchers: mutual suspicion between the sexes and the sexual double standard, which have educational consequences.

Nice girls don't

The lads in Hammertown (Willis 1977:43–6) held sexist beliefs about women. They operated a double standard between the steady girlfriend (virtuous and sexually faithful) and the 'easy lay' (cheap and promiscuous). One of his informants claimed that 'once they've had it, they want it all the time, no matter who it's with' so that the 'easy lay' is damned by the whole group. Willis suggests the girls have no scope to be assertive or sexual, and are forced into romantic silliness. This double standard was clearly recognized by the girls studied by Deirdre Wilson (1978), Lesley Smith (1978) and Sue Lees (1986). Wilson's sample of young women between 13 and 15 in northern England divided girls into virgins, 'nice' girls who had sex when in love with a steady, responsible boy, and 'lays' who would go with anyone. Nice girls avoided friendships with 'lays' because association with a bad girl could tarnish their own reputation. Lesley Smith's sample of 14 to 16 year olds in Bristol held similar views, even when they doubted the justice of them. For example:

> Liz: Look I don't believe there should be one standard for a boy and another for a girl. But there just is round here and there's not much you can do about it. A chap's going to look for someone who hasn't had it off with every bloke. So as soon as you let him put a leg over you, you've got a bad name.

Similarly, Sue Lees (1986) was told a decade later:

> When there're boys talking and you've been out with more than two you're known as the crisp that they're passing around. . . . The boy's alright but the girl's a bit of scum. (p.40)

Girls have to avoid being 'slags' themselves, and they must not associate with other girls who have bad reputations. Lees was told:

> If someone for whatever reason has got a bad name. . . can't go with that girl. Because you get called the same name and if you're hanging around with a slag you must be one. (p.49)

Adolescent girls are careful to maintain their reputations as 'nice' girls and avoid being labelled 'slags' and 'sluts'. The latter can be spotted by a variety of signs, but one of them, in the boys' eyes, is a girl's knowledge and use of contraceptives. Teenage girls know that if they reveal any experience with contraception they will be labelled as 'tarts' and treated accordingly. In the girls' eyes, it is socially reasonable to risk pregnancy rather than be labelled a 'tart'. Studies on health and sex education (e.g. Rocheron 1985, Measor 1989) in comprehensive schools reveal that teachers do not challenge these adolescent beliefs. It is likely that if teenage pregnancy (Murcott 1980), and even more importantly the spread of AIDS, are to be prevented, teachers will have to find some way of persuading boys to rethink their double standard, and of encouraging girls to risk social ostracism and preserve their health. Aggleton *et al.* (1988, 1989) discuss these issues specifically in relation to AIDS.

There is also the controversial issue of adolescents' confusions about male sexuality and sexual orientation. For most adolescents any boy who cannot, or does not, fight, run, jump and struggle to be *macho* is labelled as 'soft', and even as a 'pouf', 'boff' or 'fruit'. (See Delamont and Galton 1986, Best 1983, Measor and Woods 1984.) These insults, which are *not* based on evidence of an adult male's homosexual orientation developing, are desperately hurtful for the adolescent boy, gay or straight. Boys who went to Maid Marion School in Bridgehampton objected to wearing the uniform blazers and ties because they were unmanly:

> Irving: The things I don't like about Maid Marion. . . . Having to wear school uniforms because you look a puff (*sic*).
> Jerome: Things I dislike about Maid Marion are. . . .Having to wear a school uniform is another things (*sic*) I dislike because we look like "BOFFS".

Masculinity is very precarious!

If teachers systematically challenged pupils' simplistic ideas about male and female behaviour, and presented a clear vision of a world in which *all* skills and personal qualities are associated with both sexes and irrelevant to sexual orientation, then such insults would have no force. (See Connell (1987), for a fuller treatment of these ideas.) A boy who prefers reading to cross-country running, or sewing to soccer has a right to his preferences, and schools should cherish and encourage them.

These beliefs about sexuality may not seem immediately relevant to education. Yet the magazine *Honey* in June and July 1977 published a survey of 190 unmarried women between 18 and 26 about their sexual activities and attitudes. This survey showed clear differences between the regions of Britain, between the classes, and, noticeably, by education. Women who had stayed on at school to do A-levels had significantly different patterns of sexual behaviour and attitudes. Such women were less likely to be sexually experienced than early leavers. Once the women who stay on at school or college to do A-levels had experienced sexual relations they were more likely to use contraceptives (97 per cent) than those who were early leavers. The difference between 'stayers' and 'leavers' is clear enough, and supports earlier work of a more scholarly kind such as Kelsall *et al.* (1972). An exception was Christine Farrell (1978) who found no class difference in sexual experience among girls, but she did not control for school attainment. Willis (1977), however, found that his 'lads' did see sexual experience as marking them off from the goody-goody 'earholes' in Hammertown. Sexual experience was associated with masculinity and maturity by the 'lads'.

There is a suggestion, then, that early sexual experience and leaving school at the minimum age are associated, and that, especially in the working class, failure to be sexually active and failure to leave school are both 'unfeminine' and 'unmasculine' respectively. Leaving school at 16 may seem a small issue, but it has far-reaching consequences for the adolescent. It is likely to affect age of marriage, earning power and sexual relationships. The actual age of marriage is definitely related to completing full-time education, for early marriage is associated with one partner being in paid employment. *Social Trends, 1988* reveals that in 1986 the average age of marriage for women was 24 years. For men, the average was 26. After dropping steadily for 20 years up till 1970, the age at which first marriage takes place for women rose again. In 1961 28 per cent of brides were under 20, whereas by 1986 only 14 per cent were. Some of the research on youth unemployment – the major social problem for this age group in the early 1980s – suggests that while *marriage* was delayed by those leaving school without qualifications, cohabitation and childbearing were not (Wallace 1987, Coffield *et al.* 1986). The distinction is clear between the earlier than average marriage or cohabitation and parenthood of the working-class 'leaver', and the later than average 'coupling' of the middle-class 'stayer-on'. There also seems to be something more nebulous that leads schools to implant in girls the idea that academic success is not feminine, and in many boys that it is 'sissy'.

Certainly the distinction between 'lads' and 'earholes' in the Willis (1977) study is their attitude to the instrumental value of education. 'Lads' wanted to enter masculine, manual jobs for which educational qualifications were not wanted, while 'earholes' wanted qualifications for their careers. In other words, 'lads' rejected both the instrumental and symbolic values of education. Willis (1977:96) describes the 'lads' ' idea of a job:

> The future work situation has to have an essentially masculine ethos. It has to be a place where people are not 'cissies' and can 'handle themselves', where 'pen pushing' is looked down on in favour of really 'doing things'. . . . The . . . job must pay good money quickly.

Later Willis elaborates this by saying that 'physical labouring comes to stand for and express, most importantly, a kind of masculinity . . . a kind of machismo'(p.104). Research such as that by Hargreaves (1967), Parker (1974) and Willis at least shows a logic and consistency among those working-class boys who reject school. The study by Connell and his co-workers in Australia (1982) is a sensitive exploration of the same processes. (See also Walker, 1988).)

The lack of 'ambition' among girls, especially working-class ones, is under-researched and still not understood. Study after study has found that girls like school much more than boys do (e.g. Dove 1975) and miss the social relationships they have there when they leave (Coffield *et al.* 1986). Between 1945 (when girls began to get an equal chance at secondary qualifications) and the end of the 1970s, boys left school with more qualifications than girls, and fewer girls stayed on in education after the legal leaving age. The 1980s saw this reversed. *Social Trends 19* (1989:55) compares male and female school leavers' qualifications in Scotland, England and Wales in 1975 and 1986, reproduced here as table 3.1. This reveals that the percentage of teenagers leaving school without any exam passes fell sharply, so that only 13 per cent of boys and 9 per cent of girls are now totally unqualified. Among the pupils who left school at 16, girls have better results than boys; more girls than boys enter sixth forms, and those who do A-levels or 'Highers' are performing equally well there. So it is no longer the case that young women

Table 3.1 School leavers' highest qualifications by sex 1975–6 and 1986–7 compared

Percentage with:	Boys		Girls	
	1975–6	1986–7	1975–6	1986–7
2 or more A-levels/ 3 or more H-grades	14.3	15.0	12.1	14.7
1 A-level/or 2 H-grades	3.5	3.6	4.0	4.2
5 or more O-levels/grades at A–C (no A-levels)	7.2	9.5	9.4	11.8
1–4 O-levels/grades at A-C	23.9	24.7	27.0	29.2
1 or more 0-levels/grades D or E, or CSE grade 2-5	29.9	34.5	28.4	31.0
No GCE/SCE or CSE grades	21.2	12.7	19.1	9.1
	100.0	100.0	100.0	100.0
Total school leavers	423,000	442,000	400,000	425,000

are underperforming in schools. There is still a major distinction between the performance of the sexes in terms of the subjects they study. Girls still predominate in modern languages and biology, boys in physical sciences and technologies.

There is, then, a sense in which we know why many working-class boys reject school, even if we do not know what, if anything, can be done about it. We do not, however, know why working-class girls, who are *less openly hostile* to school, continue to opt for leaving without any qualifications that will support them economically. Boys such as those studied by Willis (1977) seem to have a realistic perception of their future in the labour market, while the girls who are their equivalents do not seem to realize that they will have to work for most of their lives in badly paid, unskilled jobs unless they leave school with qualifications, *even if they marry*. The rosy glow of romance seems to blind adolescent girls to the realities of the labour market and schools have not begun to find ways to make them face reality.

Holland (1988) summarizes the Girls and Occupational Choice (GAOC) Project, which followed a sample of London state school pupils through from 11 to 16. The findings are depressing. Boys and girls narrow and restrict their ambitions and expectations as they move towards the school leaving age, retreating into stereotyped 'masculine' and 'feminine' roles. Girls particularly 'scale down' their earlier aspirations, claiming they are not clever enough for their original choices. Being feminine leads to jobs in the female ghetto. The respondent to earlier work done by the same team, who said 'I would like to be a vet, but I expect I'll be a mother', summarizes the female mixture of resignation and resistance to the aims of schools.

In the next section the ways in which schools treat the sexes are examined, to see how masculine and feminine roles are reinforced.

Sex stereotyping in ordinary schools

It is very hard to recognize all the ways in which perfectly ordinary schools segregate, differentiate and even discriminate against some pupils on the basis of their sex. We all grew up in schools that divided us by sex, and we are all liable to perpetuate sexual divisions because we simply do not notice them. When some of the ways in which schools are sexually divisive are mentioned they seem trivial; others are seen as 'natural' and both labels prevent change. This section uses data from several studies of schools to illustrate ways in which sexual differentiation and discrimination take place, and then explains why they matter and how they can be changed. The five main arenas for sexual divisions in schools discussed are: school organization, teacher control, lesson content and structure, and informal teacher pupil relations and pupils' own stereotyping. In all these areas of school life many teachers are teaching sex-role behaviour by default, because they are stereotyping and segregating the sexes. The lessons about sex roles which are reinforced by organizational and managerial arrangements may not be those which staff want pupils to learn at all.

School organization

The Sex Discrimination Act of 1975 included several clauses which were designed to stop schools offering different subjects or organizational arrangements to males and females. Yet schools observed in 1977/8 and in 1985/6 were breaking the law and organizing boys and girls into separate subjects. In 1978 Waverly School in Coalthorpe (an industrial city in the North of England) offered woodwork and metalwork only to boys, and only girls did needlework and cookery (Delamont and Galton 1986). 'n South Wales in 1986 two schools visited, Derllwyn and fynnon Frenhines, taught all the crafts in single-sex groups, and boys and girls did different subjects. At Derllwyn all the pupils observed were in single-sex and single-ability groups for craft, so the boys from Mr Whaddon's second-year 'remedial and statemented' group did woodwork and metalwork, while the girls did needlework and cookery. This sex differentiation was also found at Ffynnon Frenhines. At a third school, Llanddewi, only boys did metalwork and woodwork, although both sexes got some 'survival' cookery. At Brynhenlog, girls did 'typing' in a single-sex group while boys did 'keyboard skills' in an all-male class. Thus at Derllwyn and Ffynnon Frenhines, boys never learnt to cook themselves a meal or sew on a button; while at Ffynnon Frenhines, Derllwyn and Llanddewi the girls got no chance to handle tools, use lathes or work with wood or metal. Apart from such striking examples of illegal curriculum segregation, there are many other ways in which schools are organized that separate, stereotype and divide the pupils.

The sex-stereotyped organization in nine South Wales schools in 1985/6 was similar to that found in 1977/8 by the ORACLE project (Delamont 1980, Galton and Willcocks 1983, Delamont and Galton 1986). Carol Buswell (1981) saw that pupils were divided by sex about twenty times every day in a Newcastle comprehensive, like the nine Welsh schools. Pupils were listed separately on the register, went into assembly in single-sex lines, waited outside classrooms in single-sex lines, had separate PE, used different cloakrooms, changing rooms and lavatories, ate lunch in different sittings, and so on. During the teachers' industrial action of 1985–6, sometimes only one sex was sent home. Boys and girls also wore different clothing. Several schools enforced ties and blazers for boys and not girls, or made girls wear skirts rather than trousers and so on. In organizational terms, the sexes were frequently separated and differentiated for administrative convenience, not for educational reasons. Of all the above separations only the changing rooms and lavatories would receive widespread public support. Outside schools females wear trousers, eat at the same tables as males, and hang their coats on neighbouring hooks without any comment. Two brief examples will illustrate these points. At Llanddewi, the first-and second-year children ate lunch at a different sitting from older children, and were further divided by sex, so that all the girls had lunch together, and then all the boys. Pupils of low ability (all statemented children) from Mrs Lavater's special class which we were observing were therefore separated from one another, so that the three girls went to the first sitting, and the boys were sent in later. Each set of children was observed mixing in the dining queue and at tables with friends from other classes – but never with children of the opposite sex. This is an organizational arrangement which segregates the sexes, and discourages them from interacting socially.

Listing the two sexes separately on the register may seem a neutral act. However if the register is used to organize classrooms serious consequences can arise. At both Waverly and Melin Court (schools in Coalthorpe) the boys were listed first on the register and this had a consequence in technical drawing at Waverly and in woodwork at Melin Court. The ORACLE observers wrote:

> After break go to Technical Drawing with Mr. Quill. He lines them up at the back and the side of the room, and allocates seats in alphabetical order. Boys first – leaving spaces for absentees. There are twenty eight children on the class list – and only twenty three proper drawing tables – so five girls get left without proper desks and are given slots on the side benches. Then they are told that when anyone is absent, they can sit in the absentees' seats. (Waverly)

> In the woodwork room the new pupils are being allocated

places at the benches in alphabetical order, with the boys first. When Mr. Beech found that he had twenty three in the group it was girls left without bench places – about three girls left to work in any space left where someone was absent (i.e. changing seats each lesson/starting each lesson by trying to find a bench space to work at). (Melin Court)

Here the use of a sex-segregated register had two consequences: sex-segregated seating in the technical drawing classroom and woodwork room, and inducing a feeling of unease and 'non-belonging' in girls. I am sure the masters did not mean to make the female pupils feel insecure in their rooms, but using the register to organize seating had that effect.

Some schools and teachers are still subverting formal arrangements by informal practices. At an inner-city school studied by Gillborn (1987) in the 1980s, when the mixed third-year class were being told about their post-14 option choices, one science master was clearly planning for all-male science groups in the fourth and fifth year. Gillborn reports:

> Mr Flint shouted across at a group of girls, at the back of the class, to stop talking. He had already succeeded in quietening them with 'I haven't got all day to wait for you lot'. However, he went on very aggressively, 'ONE THING I HATE AND DETEST IS IGNORANT FEMALES ... AND THIS SCHOOL IS LOUSY WITH THEM THESE DAYS. Suppose I'd better address myself to you lads. Don't want to see that ugly lot in my lab'.

Only a brave and self-confident girl would have chosen physics and chemistry after that.

School organization is not neutral, even when we take it for granted. Constantly separating pupils by sex emphasizes sex differences, and when male and female pupils are occasionally required to co-operate they find it very difficult (Elliot 1974, Barnes and Todd 1977, Tann 1981, Delamont and Galton 1986, Best 1983).

Motivation and control

The ORACLE team found teachers using gender differentiation as a way of motivating and controlling pupils. Using ridicule to enforce discipline was also common. For example, when Miss Wordsworth at Melin Court told the girls in her form to line up for Assembly and a boy, Wayne, stood up, she said 'Oh Wayne thinks he's a girl'. Wayne sat down again immediately. Abraham's (1989a) fieldwork in a comprehensive in the south of England in 1986 says:

> Disruptive boys would be made to sit with the girls on the assumption that that would keep the boys quiet. (p.70)

Attempting to motivate boys to work by comparing them to girls was frequently seen. For example:

> At Waverly Miss Southey had a class in the school library and when she saw most of the girls had borrowed books but none of the boys she said 'All the girls are taking out books but not one boy yet. Can't the boys read in this class?'.

A few boys then borrowed books but most did not, despite the teacher's comment. Similar teacher strategies were common in nine Welsh schools in 1985/6 both to maintain order or organize activities for which no educational reason existed. For example at Gwaelod-y-Garth the fourth-year remedial and statemented group had a rural studies lesson in which the boys were sent out, unsupervised, to wheel some barrow loads of earth to a new flower bed while the master interviewed the girls and filled in their assessment profiles with them. As only one girl could be seen at once, and the others were left to chat, they could have been moving the earth with the boys. The sex segregation served no educational purpose, only an organizational one. A common teacher control strategy was to allow one sex to leave the room before the other. Thus, in Mrs Leithen's class at Gwaelod-y-Garth:

> It is 3.30. Mrs. Leithen says 'Nobody is going from here till you are all quiet'. When they are quiet they are allowed to leave a small number at a time, girls first, then the boys in

small groups.

This may work as a control strategy, but at the cost of emphasizing that boys and girls are different, and reinforcing their own prejudices. At Derllwyn when the Senior Mistress of the Lower School was doing a history lesson on Pompeii with the remedial and statemented first years she found that Royden was doing nearly all the answering, so she suggested, 'Let's ask the girls for a change'. When the class moved on to RE Royden again volunteered answers to most of the questions and this teacher too suggested that, 'Now the girls in front are sitting awful quiet'. Here again the reasonable teacher strategy – getting other pupils to share in the progress of the lesson – is realized in a sex-segregating way. Other pupils are 'girls' – not individuals – and the other boys in the class were equally unresponsive to the teacher's questions and needed to be encouraged to answer. Singling out 'girls' serves only to reinforce their difference from Royden and other boys, 'shows them up' and does nothing to encourage all the other pupils to participate in the discourse.

Teaching strategies and lesson content

The content of much of the curriculum, and the ways in which teachers taught the material is also full of sex stereotyping. Carol Buswell (1981) analysed the lower-school humanities materials. There were 326 pages of text, including 169 pictures of men and only 21 of women, and 102 individual men were described as against 14 women. Among the tasks for pupils were the following:

(1) Look at the pictures of the clothes the Romans wore. Would they be easy for your mother to wash if you were a Roman?
(2) Find the name of this make of car. Your father or brother will probably know, ask them.
(3) Make up a poem about a very rich man or a very poor man.

Winter (1983) has highlighted the restricted number of female characters in reading materials for slow learners in the second-ary age range, and the limited range of occupations and low ambitions the women characters have. Frances James, a remedial teacher, made the same point in a letter to the *Guardian* (17 February 1987).

Sexual stereotyping was also common in the textbooks, worksheets and teaching in the Welsh schools. So for example at Ffynnon Frenhines when the second year were doing an exercise on healthy eating with Mrs Barralty, she discovered that none of the children knew what stock was.

> Mrs. Barralty asked 'What's in a stock? Come on, girls, you do cookery . . .'.
> Vaughan replies 'OXO'.

This interaction was doubly interesting. It confirmed for the observer that all the staff knew boys did not do cookery at Ffynnon Frenhines, and stereotyped the girls. As a boy (Vaughan) was the only child in the room to have any idea how gravy was made, so the teacher's expectation was confounded. At Heol y Crynwyr, a school where most activities were integrated, stereotyped curriculum materials were in use. For example, in Mr Arcoll's laboratory the walls were decorated with posters. One faded set featured boys and girls doing dangerous things in the lab and being reprimanded by an adult. Another series, published by the Royal Society of Chemistry, on 'Achievements in Chemistry', included five posters, four of males, one the Curies. The Equal Opportunities Commission (EOC) posters of women scientists (see Smail 1984:38) were *not* displayed.

Abraham (1989a) has provided a detailed analysis of the textbooks and materials used in English, French and maths in 1986 in one comprehensive. He concluded that the textbooks in maths and French were male dominated, with men in the powerful and active roles and females in stereotyped 'feminine' ones. One maths book defines 'a mathematician' as male, and another includes the inaccurately sexist claim that:

> If the government says that the unemployment rate is 6% they mean that averaged over the whole country six out of every 100 *men* are unemployed.

Such bias in teaching materials is carried through into exams. The Fawcett Society (see Hendry 1987) studied all the 1985 GCE papers in maths, physical sciences, computing, languages, history and social sciences. Maths papers were replete with 'workmen', 'foremen' and men investing money as well as problems about engines and football. The science and computing papers were 'impersonal', but across 250 papers 22 different, famous male scientists were named but only one woman (Marie Curie's death). English literature exams focus on male characters in plays, poems and novels written by men as do the literature papers in French and German. Home economics exams provide the most blatant examples – especially the practical test:

> Your brother has a Saturday job at a local farm. (a) Prepare and pack a substantial midday meal for him to take and make a family supper dish. (b) Launder his shirt and trousers, clean and press his jacket and clean his shoes ready for a disco in the evening. (Hendry 1987:37)

As the researcher concludes, boys are 'rigorously excluded' from the home economics papers, except as recipients of women's labour.

The stereotyping in texts and materials is particularly damaging because pupils have a 'blind spot' concerning the use of the words 'man' and 'men' to mean human beings rather than just males. This is a common flaw in teaching materials and in the oral parts of lessons. There is ample research evidence that pupils and students hear 'man' to mean 'males' unless they are explicitly told that it covers people of both sexes. There are forty-four articles on this point in Thorne et al. (1983), including Schneider and Hacker (1973) who found undergraduates studying social science interpreted 'men' in that way and Harrison (1975) who reports adolescents making the same mistake studying 'the evolution of man'. Teachers need to explain to pupils, especially those who are low-achievers, that 'man's evolution' means human evolution, and 'great men of science' includes Marie Curie, Rosalind Franklin and Barbara McClintock, but few currently do so.

There are authors who claim that teachers allow boys to

dominate the talk in classrooms, taking three-quarters of all the teacher's attention and making three-quarters of the pupil contributions (e.g. Spender 1982; see also Delamont 1984c). Such claims do not stand up to close scrutiny because there are too few data to make them. However, studies do show differences in the ways teachers respond to male and female pupils. Shuy's (1986) analysis of a high school civics lesson taught by William Bennett (at the time Reagan's Secretary of State for Education) showed he regularly challenged things his male pupils said ('why did you say that?') but never the responses from his female pupils. The girls got positive or neutral feedback ('Okay', 'Alright', 'Very nice', 'Terrific'). (See also Delamont (1986) on this lesson.) A great deal more research is needed on this area, but all teachers can tape themselves and examine whether they are treating the boys and girls in their rooms differently and, if so, in what ways.

Sometimes teachers try to avoid sexism but are frustrated by others. At Ffynnon Frenhines we saw the girls from the 'remedial and statemented' class join one of the 'B' band forms for PE. The teacher, Mrs Varrinder, sent those girls who had forgotten their kit down from the upstairs gym to the downstairs one, where the boys were having PE, to fetch back the benches that were normally kept there which had been 'borrowed' before half term. They returned empty handed, followed by boys carrying the benches, detailed by the PE master, who had been teaching male PE in the main hall. Mrs Varrinder's attempt to get some girls to carry benches was frustrated by the PE master, who chivalrously assigned boys to do it for them, stressing female dependence. Some of the boys assigned were smaller than the girls they were 'helping'!

Teacher-pupil banter

When teachers engage in informal interactions with pupils they may inadvertently be reinforcing stereotyped sex roles. Classroom jokes may also be based on sexual stereotypes, and so are many attempts to make lesson content relevant and immediate to pupils:

The top French set are in the language lab, and the pupils were answering questions in French about their families. A boy who says he has four sisters gets the cheery comment from the master 'Poor Lad'. (*Waverly*)

One day at Derllwyn the first-year boys were scheduled for woodwork, but because they had been so badly behaved in the workshop in previous lessons the master took them to the graphics (TD) room, to design a poster instead. While discussing how a 'For Sale' poster should be designed the master said: 'if I was selling a car to a woman I'd put the colour first'. (That is, before the make, price or mileage.) Such stereotyped comments served only to reinforce sexual prejudices that pupils already have.

Riddell (1989:188) studied two comprehensives in Southwest England from 1983 to 1985. In history at Greenhill Mr Stanhope 'explained' Bloody Mary's persecution of Protestants by saying she was forced to stay unmarried, and went on to ask the girls to empathize with her:

When you leave school you may have a career and you may want to return to it afterwards, but still at the heart of your lives will be getting married and having children. It's the most natural thing in the world despite what some feminists might like to say.

In the same school, Mr Hill, a physics teacher, humanized electricity by asking the class to imagine the boys were negative charges and the girls were positive charges.

They all knew, he said, that girls tended to run after boys, but were nasty to other girls, and of course boys did not like each other unless they were queer. This analogy was used for several weeks, interspersed with comments about queers and fruity boys, and was even extended to the description of an ammeter as a dirty old man standing on the street corner counting girls going by.

Riddell says these were extreme examples, but outweighed the even smaller number of lessons which challenged stereotypes. One woodwork master at Millbridge was honest enough to tell

Riddell that having mixed classes cramped his style because he had enjoyed sharing dirty jokes with the boys, and how 'if you've got girls there . . .you've got to watch your language' (p.189).

Jokes would not be a source of sex stereotyping if all other aspects of schooling were more thoroughly egalitarian and free of sex segregation, sex differentiation and sex discrimination.

The pupils' view

Adolescent pupils have just the same stereotypes and triple standards as younger children, but these are complicated by the developing sense of sexuality, the heightened importance of peer group pressures, and acute self-consciousness. Measor (1984, 1989) is a particularly sensitive chronicler of these issues. The miseries of school life between 12 and 16 are well captured in this letter to *Woman* (3 July 1989).

> They Tease Me
> Last week I was on the school bus, and some boys in my class stole my bag. Before I could stop them, they'd opened the side pocket and found my tampons. I just burst into tears and got off at the next stop. Now they all laugh and tease me, calling me Little Miss Tampon. Please help me. I hate school and sometimes I want to kill myself.

This encapsulates many of the findings of research on being an adolescent girl in general and managing menstruation in particular (Prendergast 1989). Boys are equally under pressure to shape up as men, as the desperate letter from KK (chapter 1) showed. In Canaan's (1986, 1987) work on young people in Sheepshead, an American suburban community, being a high-status male pupil means not being a 'wimp' or 'faggot' which has little to do with sexuality, but everything to do with aggressive, *macho* self-presentation, particularly at sport. So Jack is 'such a fag' just because he cried in class when a teacher asked why he had not handed in his homework. Canaan's teenagers had all the same double standards about sexuality, and all the same stereotypes about male and female roles that

British researchers have found. In Britain the boy who does not finish the cross-country run is a 'boff' or 'fruity boy', the girl who wears the 'wrong' type of skirt to school is a slut. Anyone who suggests that males and females can be friends, or that boys might like art better than metalwork, or that a girl could aspire to be an airline pilot risks ostracism in most schools. Abraham (1989b) studied a group of boys who rejected traditional roles, and they were scorned not only by traditional boys but by some teachers, who complained that they were 'effeminate' and 'softly spoken like a girl' (p.79).

There is considerable evidence that male pupils regard most female teachers as 'soft' compared to men, and may even sexually harass them. (See for example Riddell 1989, Connell *et al.* 1982; Beynon 1987 and 1989.) Overall, pupils have, by adolescence, become deeply embedded in sexist stereotypes, which schools do little or nothing to challenge. However, there is some evidence that by the mid-1980s adolescent girls were beginning to envisage a less sex-segregated future for themselves, while boys in the same schools were not. Lois Weis (1989) reports this from a depressed industrial area in America where:

> Boys still envision a patriarchal future – one in which they are the breadwinners and their wives stay at home taking care of the children. They envision patriarchy in its rather strict sense of *separate spheres*. . . .The girls are attempting. . .to break the present-day manifestation of patriarchy.

Similar findings have come out of research on how fear of AIDS is affecting adolescents' sexual perspectives: girls are taking the impact of AIDS seriously, boys are not changing their behaviour at all.

The picture outlined is a negative one and may have left the reader feeling depressed about schools and schooling. In the fifth chapter some solutions and proposals for change are discussed.

4 The teachers

> Though most social science is indeed about men, good quality research that brings *masculinity* into focus is rare. . . .The political meaning of writing about masculinity turns mainly on its treatment of power. . . . It is necessary to face the facts of sexual power without evasion but also without simplification. . . . The analysis of masculinity needs to be related as well to other currents in feminism. Particularly important are those that have focused on the sexual division of labour, the sexual politics of workplaces, and the interplay of gender relations with class dynamics.
>
> (Carrigan *et al.* 1987:64)

These men are writing about males in general, but their argument is especially applicable to a chapter reviewing research on teachers. Connell (1985) has conducted sensitive research on gender and teaching which focuses on both sexes. This chapter covers teachers and their views on sex roles in the school. It begins with a consideration of recruitment to teaching, and the ideas and beliefs of entrants. This is followed by a consideration of how practising teachers handle sex roles in the staffroom and classroom. Promotions and careers are discussed next, to see who is successful in reaching top jobs and why. Then the consequences of these various features of teaching are briefly examined. The focus of this chapter, on how teachers view and act concerning sex roles, means that many studies of teachers and teaching are not considered. The research on how teachers work in classrooms is reviewed in Delamont (1987a) and Atkinson *et al.* (1988b). Other aspects of the occupation are covered in Ball (1987), Denscombe (1985), Ball and Goodson

(1984), Sikes *et al.* (1985) and Lawn and Grace (1987).

It is, however, striking that while there has been an increase in studies of practising teachers in the 1980s, and several authors (see Acker 1989, Nias 1989, De Lyon and Migniuolo 1989) have begun to produce work on women teachers, our knowledge of teaching has large gaps in it. There are very few studies of how teachers are socialized into the occupation (see Atkinson and Delamont 1985a) and none of masculinity and teaching. These are serious gaps when considering teachers' ideas about sex roles, and their role in challenging or reinforcing those held by colleagues and pupils.

Who enters teaching?

The research on the social background of teachers has shown that most come from lower-middle- and upper-working-class backgrounds, and that the women tend to have 'better' social origins than the men. Also, studies have shown that teachers in academically and socially 'select' schools come from higher-status backgrounds than those in ordinary state schools (Lacey 1977). There are good historical reasons for these recruitment patterns which are discussed in Tropp (1957). In this section the focus is on the kinds of people who become teachers, and the ideas they have about sex roles.

Teachers are produced by the higher education system, and so potential teachers are a minority of young people, for the vast majority of school leavers do not enter higher education. *Social Trends 1989* (pp. 58–9) shows that in 1986/7 only 25 per cent of people aged 18–24 were still in full-time education: 6 per cent in polytechnics and colleges, 4 per cent in universities, and the rest in further education colleges. Student numbers in full-time higher education have risen since 1980/1, because more people are going to polytechnics and colleges and because more women are entering higher education. In 1980/1 58 per cent of students were men, but in 1986/7 only 54 per cent were. By 1986/7 there were 134,300 male graduates from universities and 101,400 women, with another 145,300 males and 137,100 females graduating from polytechnics and colleges. Women were obtaining 44 per cent of the first degrees. These 520,000 graduates are a minority of their age group (10 per cent), and it is from this small population that teachers come.

The bare figures do not tell us which students will enter teaching, nor anything about their attitudes and values, and unfortunately we have little or no research on contemporary sixth formers or students. Smithers and Hill (1989) have recently asked sixth formers about their attitudes to entering school teaching as a career. Teaching was not seen as a good job by most of their sample as the following quotes show:

> I think the pay is abominable. I think the way children treat teachers is abominable. The work they have to do is a lot for the money they get. They have got degrees yet they are not appreciated at all.

> Bad pay, extremely boring, simply repeating work annually, controlled by headmaster.

> The wages are very poor and I don't like children.

Only 3 per cent of the males and 12 per cent of the females felt teaching was a very good job.

Research in South Wales (Bright 1987) suggests that contemporary teachers are not encouraging sixth formers to train as teachers. He asked 144 male and female teachers on (voluntary) in-service courses whether they would advise 'a good male/female A-level candidate' to enter teaching. Only 19 per cent would advise a male sixth former to be a teacher, and only 31 per cent a female one. Teaching is still seen as a reasonable job for a woman and a poor one for a man. Hilsum and Start (1974:253) asked a sample of teachers whether they would encourage their own children to become teachers. While more than two-thirds of the sample said they would encourage a daughter to teach, over three-quarters would *not* encourage a son to do so. Male and female teachers were equally likely to encourage a daughter into their own occupation, but women were more hostile to their sons entering teaching than men were.

In the early 1990s there will be a shortage of recruits to teaching, and yet there is very little research on who *does* choose the occupation, and what their views are on important social issues. In Britain, we do not know how students in general and student teachers in particular conceptualize sexual politics or sex equality. There is no systematic research on the ideas about sex roles which recruits to teaching have apart from Galloway (1973) discussed below. We have some evidence about the division of labour by sex and the sex roles usual in the kinds of families from which teachers come. Men teachers come predominantly from skilled manual working-class homes and lower-middle- class ones, and these are precisely the kind of homes in which segregation of sex roles is common, and strong ideas about different behaviour for men and women are held. For example, the classic study of a mining town *Coal is our Life* by Dennis *et al.* (1957) showed rigidly segregated sex roles, and males and females leading separate lives. Incidents recorded in 'Ashton' suggest that there was a strong tradition of all men combining to keep women in their place – out of the pub, the club and the betting office – and considerable hostility between men and women, except during courtship. The period captured in *Coal is our Life* now seems very far away and long ago. However, many more recent studies of working-class and lower-middle-class households and communities (e.g. Whitehead 1976, Hill 1976, Blackburn and Mann 1979, Crehan 1986) show men and women living essentially separate lives at work and leisure, only meeting in their homes.

The majority of men teachers in British schools will have been raised in homes with segregated sex roles. Those men who have left their working-class backgrounds might have also shed their sex-role ideologies. However, it is equally plausible to suggest that those working-class males who enter the 'soft' job of teaching would cling especially firmly to their childhood ideas of separate sex roles.

More of the women entrants to teaching since 1945 have come from middle-class homes than the men. However, the majority have entered teaching via teacher training colleges, and by the very act of going to those colleges they were missing out on a general higher education which would open lots of jobs, in favour of a path into teaching. Their motives for entering teaching, and for 'choosing' the college of education route, are not well documented. However, the study by Galloway (1973) bears on the point. Her data were drawn from interviews with women in Edinburgh University and Moray House College of Education in the early 1970s and, although unrepresentative of English or Welsh students, they are rich and illuminating. Margo Galloway was interested in women's lives to date and their expectations about their future. These students held extremely conventional ideas about the role of women, the division of labour in marriage and their own futures. Evidence collected throughout the second half of the century shows that American women were scared of being seen as clever by men in case it jeopardized their social success (Komorovsky 1946, 1972). Galloway's sample felt strongly that while men did not mind women being clever and successful, they did dislike women who were 'intellectual'. Her respondents said things like 'It's very foreboding (*sic*)' and 'I don't want to be very intellectual because I don't want to be very anything' (Galloway 1973:84) and 'men don't like you to be too emancipated'. All but one of the sample said they wanted to marry, most thought marriage and motherhood their main aims in life, and most wanted a husband who was superior to them in age, intellect, earning power and judgement. Typical comments were 'Marriage would mean more to me than any career' (p.87) and 'I think the male should be dominant in any family' (p.92).

One young woman produced, the 'typical' worldview of the majority of Galloway's (1973:103) sample. She had expressed a desire to go to Turkey for visits to collect folk material but added:

> I'd like something small but nothing big. I wouldn't like to be famous or anything like that.
> Interviewer: You wouldn't like to go down in history as the woman who unearthed all the important Turkish folk tales?
> Student: I'd rather be the wife of the man who did it.

This was an extreme case, but not that extreme. The women saw the housework as their duty and did not think men should do very much around the home. A typical woman said 'I don't mind a man helping with just the dishes but nothing else. I can't stand to see a man running round the house with an apron on' (p.96). Washing clothes and bed making were seen as particularly unmanly tasks. The majority were sure that children completed a marriage, wanted two or more, and planned to stay home for 7 to 10 years with them. These women based their conventional views of the future on a belief that gender differences are grounded in biological facts, saying women made better mothers for reasons such as 'I think women are born more patient' (p.108). Women teachers who believe that they are biologically different from men are likely to believe that their girl pupils are biologically different from the boys and act accordingly.

Galloway was especially interested in why women who were technically qualified for university had chosen to attend Moray House College to train for teaching. She had expected them to hold less 'emancipated' views of women's role, and believe university was less feminine than training for primary teaching. However, this turned out not to be the case. While the majority of the university students were there as 'the next step' expected of them by their homes and schools, the college students had usually thought about what higher education they wanted. Those women who were objectively qualified for university but did not go fell into two groups. Some were committed to teaching and chose college as the best available professional training, while others were convinced that they were not intellectually capable of university work. Both groups had stood firm against all pressures on them to go to university. None of the girls reported either their schools or parents trying to stop them going on to higher education; indeed the college girls reported pressure to aim 'higher' than they themselves wished to go.

Galloway's data can be seen in the context of national surveys conducted by Andrew McPherson and his colleagues among Scottish school leavers (e.g. Jones and McPherson 1972). In the survey carried out in 1970 they found that many of the young women who chose colleges of education lacked confidence in their own academic ability and had not been the subject of parental pressure to excel academically, unlike equivalent boys. It is not clear whether McPherson's Scottish findings would apply in England and Wales. However, the evidence from Scotland would certainly suggest that the majority of female entrants to colleges, and hence teaching, were very unliberated. The following letter to the problem page of *Woman* (2 December 1978) may be more 'typical' than perhaps it looks at first glance:

> I am just approaching the time when I have to start applying to colleges and I'm confused. I think I want to be a teacher, but wonder if I'll fall in love before I've finished training and want to have children. Then I think of how many teachers are single and I don't want to end up like that!

This young woman is obviously unsure about her own future, and also holds very muddled ideas about the interrelationships of teaching, love, motherhood and marriage. She, like the women interviewed by Galloway, is very unlikely to be in favour of using schools to change traditional sex roles.

Male recruits to the profession probably hold similarly stereotyped views about sex roles, although we lack any studies on the point in the UK. Skelton and Hanson (1989) point out how little is known about gender-related issues in initial teacher training, an area of education which has been neglected by sociologists (Atkinson and Delamont 1985a). Skelton and Hanson (1989) report that even student teachers who were aware of sexism in their training course failed to 'see' it when in schools. The standard teacher training course was suffused with assumptions about male and female pupils, all of which may become self-fulfilling prophecies (see Good 1987). In some teacher training courses, gender is covered in the 'theory' part of the syllabus, rather than in the 'methods' or 'classroom practice' sector, and can be dismissed as 'theory' rather than being seen as a crucial element in everyday classroom behaviour.

In short, it seems that most recruits to teaching have had, and will have, conventional ideas about sex roles and little is done to change these during initial training (Equal Opportunities Commission 1989). Of course, some will enter with courses in women's studies or sex roles behind them, and some will be members of women's liberation, men against sexism, or gay liberation groups. What happens to radical ideas when the teacher gets into school?

Reality shock

There is evidence (e.g. Lacey 1977) that student teachers with libertarian or progressive ideas find even their training courses and teaching practice hard to take. Lacey suggests that radical education students are likely to be forced out of teaching. Grace (1972) wrote sensitively of the problems facing the new teacher in the urban school, who has been 'carefully separated from the majority of his peers during adolescence' and is 'likely to experience shock at the realities of the inner urban classroom' (p.62). The world which has seemed normal and ordered, because it was an exclusive world in terms of class, ability and race, suddenly seems 'pathological'. Grace says 'above all, it is threatening in the very low regard which its members give to his status as teacher . . . and to the academic specialism. . . .' He continues that radical young teachers face the 'greatest contradictions' (p.63). While they may feel themselves as 'messengers essentially of human liberation and of the potentially transforming effects of critical consciousness' (p.63), their audience is unlikely to be receptive. Grace argued that many working-class parents and pupils interpret the teacher's libertarian ideas as 'softness', a finding reported also by Connell (1985).

Whiteside *et al.* (1969) made a similar point about graduate entrants to teaching and their experience of 'reality shock'. The authors surveyed 157 graduates training for secondary teaching, and suggest that those student teachers who are most traditionally academic are those who find adjusting to ordinary schools most difficult for precisely the reasons spelt out by Grace. Whiteside *et al.* found that student teachers who did not enter teaching were likely to believe that practising teachers use traditional methods and hold authoritarian ideas. They argue that student teachers face a process of 'reality shock' as they 'slowly face up to entry into the profession'. While their study did not consider attitudes to sex roles among student teachers, those with unconventional ideas would feel at odds with the majority of the occupation for which they are training.

A slightly later study of students in a college of education preparing for primary teaching shows the *process* of reality shock as it happens. Hanson and Herrington (1976a, b) followed sixteen new teachers who trained between 1970 and 1973 into the schools to see how they were licked into shape by colleagues and pupils. They concluded that 'teachers are more influenced by current school practices rather than by their professional and academic education' (1976a:568). They report on the conservative influences of the older teachers, and the explicit role pupils take in shaping new teachers into familiar patterns. If pupils and older colleagues try to train new teachers into established ways over such things as Christmas decorations in each classroom, deviations from conventional behaviour about sex roles are likely to be much more heavily punished. Teachers who hold 'progressive' ideas about gender roles would find these just as untenable in schools as other libertarian notions (Cunnison 1989, Joyce 1987).

There are some autobiographical accounts by British feminist teachers (e.g. Elliot 1978, Maciuszko 1978, Joyce 1987). Middleton (1989) has conducted life history interviews with feminist teachers in New Zealand, like Connell's (1985) research in Australia. These all show how hostile to feminism most staffrooms are, a finding supported by one survey. Kelly (1985b) has conducted a large-scale survey of British teachers and found that women teachers were more favourable to sex equality than men, and graduates more 'feminist' than college-trained teachers. Home economics teachers were the least feminist, followed by CDT, maths and science staff. People teaching humanities were the most pro-feminist. These three factors (sex, qualifications and subject taught) are all interrelated; not one graduate woman CDT teacher replied to Kelly's survey. Teachers in London were more feminist than those in other large cities. The most striking finding was that believing in the equality of the sexes as an abstract principle (a belief endorsed by nearly all teachers) does *not* imply that a teacher accepts any of the conclusions of books such as this one, or has any commitment to scrutinizing their own school for bias in texts, exams, facilities, classroom interaction or career structures.

Research on staffroom relationships shows what pressures are likely to be put upon teachers by their colleagues. Woods

(1979:230-1) recounts how a radical teacher was pressured by the headmaster and resigns from the school. From the rest of Woods' material on the staffroom at Lowfield, it is clear that the male teachers there would have little patience with feminism. Beynon (1987) found similar pressures brought to bear on a female drama teacher, Miss Floral, who wanted to explore humanistic, caring, expressive values in a tough boys' school.

The teacher who wants to change the ways in which schools structure sex roles for staff and pupils is liable to suffer the same reality shock as teachers with any other non-traditional ideas. The processing by which teachers come to be socialized into the norms and values of their colleagues has not been thoroughly studied in Britain, but there are obviously two arenas in which reality forces itself upon the young teacher, the classroom and the staffroom. The two previous chapters have shown how pupils hold their own ideas about what sex roles should be and reject many teacher attempts to challenge them. For example, when the teacher studied by Beynon (1985a) asked what drama was about, a boy answered 'Drama is girls dancing about, Miss'. This was a direct challenge to the teacher's definition of drama and its importance in a boys' school. The previous chapters have not, however, looked at how staffroom interactions about pupils and other matters focus upon sex and gender, and it is to this we now turn.

Staffroom talk

One important part of staffroom talk is the establishment and maintenance of pupils' reputations (Delamont 1984c, Hargreaves *et al.* 1975). The male staffroom 'humour' about pupils quoted by Woods (1979:223-4) shows female pupils being treated as sex objects. One conversation focused mainly on the colour of the girls' knickers and contains comments like 'My girls are dead worried. I told them they'd have to take everything off on Monday, and I hoped none of them were tattooed, and I think they believed me!' followed by 'That wouldn't worry *my* lot. They'd be only too willing to oblige'. (p.224). Male teachers who can say such things in jest (for Woods shows how really serious issues were not joking matters) are unlikely to tolerate other staff wanting to break down sexism.

How far male and female teachers carry ideas about segregated sex roles into their staffroom lives and into their judgements about pupils is unknown. However, the data collected by Hargreaves *et al.* (1975) on teachers' typifications of deviance among pupils are interesting. They comment that girls were hardly ever mentioned as 'difficult' (p.31), and the few extracts referring to girls nearly all mention talking a lot as the problem (pp.155, 227, 231). The *one* very deviant girl is explicitly singled out for the researchers because she violates appropriate feminine behaviour:

> I: Why a tomboy?
> T: When you see her knocking one or two of the boys around you know. She's not a girl I wouldn't think, she's not ladylike in any way, not at all. Her voice doesn't help. She's got a very male voice I would call it, very rusty sort of voice like mine. (p.191)

and

> T: She's a bully . . . as powerfully built as most of the boys and she'd give one or two what for now and again. (p.161)

It is not clear that this is the same girl, but a school with more than one such pupil would hardly claim that girls were not difficult. Ann Marie Wolpe (1977:39) found the equivalent case of a boy regarded askance by his teachers for a supposed lack of masculinity. In a London comprehensive school a group of pre-pubescent pupils rejected one of their cleverest form mates, Gary. On investigation the boys in his class claimed to dislike him because he was feminine. His 'femininity' consisted of sitting with the girls at lunchtime, disliking games and preferring Beethoven to pop music. Wolpe commented that:

> His obvious deviation from the desirable stereotypical masculine norm causes a measure of concern for his teachers. One in particular feels he should be referred to the Child Guidance Clinic because of his preference for Beethoven to Gary Glitter, his collection of Victoriana and his repugnance for any swearing at all.

At Waverly I was told about a rather similar pupil. One English master explicitly stated that certain other male staff could not tolerate boys who were not aggressive, rowdy and athletic but thought them 'pansies' and hence were intolerant of a boy who preferred reading poetry to football.

Apart from singling out 'masculine' girls and 'feminine' boys for censure, staffrooms are almost certainly full of beliefs about the nature of boys and girls which may or may not be 'accurate' but will certainly affect how males are handled in the school and its classrooms. Wolpe (1977:14, 38) offers two examples of beliefs about sex and gender which have obvious consequences. In one school an English master told her that he expected different kinds of written work with the girls producing 'more an airy-fairy story' while the boys were more realistic. This led him to prepare different essay titles which 'he regarded, and explicitly stated, as being eminently suitable for boys, some for girls and some neutral'. Another teacher told Wolpe that 'the boys just don't seem to get down to work or the majority of them have to be pushed. But the girls always do so'. This is a common belief, but the consequences for classroom behaviour are not known and have not been measured. Overall we need more research on how such attitudes are translated into action, both for the conformist majority of pupils and the deviant individual who is 'effeminate' or a 'tomboy' who apparently upsets most teachers.

There may be features of the occupation which accentuate any ideas teachers brought with them into the profession. Waller (1932:50) long ago pointed out that the masculinity of male teachers was perpetually in doubt, illustrating his point with the way in which swearing and bawdiness stopped when the teacher enter the barber's, just as if he were a lady. Male teachers were seen as involved with head work rather than hand work, with children rather than adults, and in an essentially feminine job rather than a masculine one. Many years later Ginsburg *et al.* (1977:34) found similar community reaction to teachers in the English Midlands.

One researcher accompanied two school B teachers to a social club (of which they were members) for a drink during the lunch hour. As we entered the bar a group of men sitting at one of the tables called out in what sounded like a heckling tone 'Hey teacher. How are you teacher?'. The two teachers acknowledged the 'greeting' with a nod and a formal smile; they seemed to be somewhat uncomfortable until we settled into a table some distance from these men . . .

This incident could almost have come from Waller, except that in his day teachers were not supposed to be seen drinking. The more general point – that male teachers are somehow 'soft' –is well captured by Sara Lawrence Lightfoot (1975):

The teacher role poses an inherent contradiction that claims that, in order to communicate effectively with children, teachers must exhibit the nurturant, receptive qualities of the female character ideal and the expressive, adaptive qualities of the child. Ironically, those same qualities are viewed as inferior and of low status when one conceives of the teacher in relation to the social and occupational structure of society.

It may be this unease which leads to the sexist micropolitics of the staffroom. Cunnison (1989) presents an analysis of this commonly reported phenomenon, also raised by Connell (1985) and Ball (1987). Woods' (1979) study of Lowfield secondary modern was one of the first to reveal how male teachers derived considerable pleasure from mocking the senior mistress, and making sexist comments about their female colleagues.

The structure of teaching

Scribbins (1977) summarizes the position of women in the profession. He says:

The teaching profession has customarily been regarded as an open profession as far as women are concerned. More women enter it than most professions and it is generally, though wrongly believed that within this profession . . . women can enter on a career trail leading to senior jobs. In fact in education in general . . . there is a clear pattern of discrimination against women . . .

Scribbins points out that the more expensive and academically high status the sector of the education system is, the fewer women there are. As we move down from higher education to the nursery school, the proportion of women rises. Additionally, within each sector there are fewer women staff in the higher salary brackets and in the senior posts. These inequalities are relatively new, having replaced different ones since 1945. Women entering school teaching, and teacher training institutions had, in 1945, the possibilities of two types of top job. They could aspire to become a headmistress, or the principal of a women's training college. Both were well-paid occupations with considerable social cachet, and led to other work – the magistrate's bench, committees, local councils and so forth. Even if one did not reach the top of these parallel trees, one could become a head of department in either a school or college. Admittedly, in 1945 there was no equal pay for women teachers, but there was a career structure. By 1985 equal pay had become legal in theory – although rarely achieved in practice – and the career structure had gone with the coming of coeducation.

Sutherland (1985) has pointed out that coeducation was adopted in England as an undiscussed adjunct to going comprehensive. No sustained public debate took place at national or local level about the consequences of coeducation for the careers of women in teaching. Yet what women teachers gained with the award of equal pay they lost with the coming of coeducation, because no provisions were made to safeguard their career ladder in the coeducational schools. Teachers only got equal pay in 1961, and in Scotland, England and Wales there existed men's unions opposed to equal pay for women up until the Sex Discrimination Act (1975) made single-sex unions illegal. The struggle for equal pay, described by Partington (1976) was long and bitter, and it should not surprise us if entrenched positions adopted during that struggle have not disappeared. The principle of equal pay in teaching was established in 1955, with a settlement then planned to phase it in over 6 years. The National Association of Schoolmasters (NAS) campaigned to have the decision reversed, while the National Union of Women Teachers (NUWT) campaigned to have equal pay adopted at once (King 1987, Corr 1987). During this period an NAS man wrote in the *Times Educational Supplement* (12

April 1957) that women only came into teaching 'to get a husband to get them out of it. The women's staff room has become a waiting room for the bridal chamber and an anteroom for the maternity home!'. Such statements can still be heard in staffrooms, alongside the verdict on women teachers quoted at the head of chapter 1. Cunnison (1989:154) reports the following:

> an assistant house head came into the staffroom with information about mock interviews to be held as a training exercise for those seeking promotion. His opposite number, a woman, asked to see the information. He handed it over but as he did so growled at her 'What do *you* want it for? Women are only fit for breeding!'.

The battle for equal pay was long – it began with a resolution put to the NUT conference of 1904 – and extremely bitter, as Partington's thorough history shows. However, it would be hard to argue that the sexual inequalities in pay and promotion which are found in school teaching and in teacher training institutions today are a legacy from that struggle. Rather the rapid spread of coeducation has, as Zimmern (1898) Davies (1937) and Clarke (1937) feared, closed the main career and promotion path for the woman teacher – in the girls' school – without providing equality in the coeducational one. Some 30 years after the principle of equal pay was gained, women teachers are clustered in the lowest-paid sectors of teaching and, within each sector, in the lower-paid parts of it. The HMI (1979) survey found that 20 per cent of senior teachers were women, 22 per cent of those on Scale 4, and 58 per cent of those on scale 1. It looks as if the sex balance is roughly equal among scale 2 teachers, and men become the majority in each promoted grade above scale 2. The NUT/EOC (1980) survey revealed a similar point when they compared the percentage of all male and female teachers who had reached promoted posts.

The everyday, and lifetime, experience of men and women secondary teachers are different. The typical man is likely to gain a promoted post; many women never rise higher than scale 2. Although today most secondary teachers in LEA schools work in coeducation, their career prospects are different. The ILEA, which maintained many single-sex schools, offered more career prospects for women teachers. Thus in 1981 the ILEA had 22 per cent of their mixed secondary schools headed by a woman, as well as 98 per cent of their girls' secondary schools – although not one boys' school had a headmistress. The 22 per cent of headships of mixed schools held by women in the ILEA was unusually large (see Wells 1985, Davidson 1985). The percentage of women who have been promoted to senior positions, especially headships, within any one LEA is an important factor in the promotion prospects of other women candidates for headships there. Morgan, Hall and Mackay (1983) found that there was a vicious circle which could prevent women becoming heads in areas which had few women headteachers already. The authors report that, in England and Wales, in the early 1980s 'the selection of headteachers is carried out in an arbitrary and amateur way' (p. 145)'.

A substantial part of the selection involves committee members matching candidates against stereotypes of heads they have encountered. 'Many more models of men headteachers are available to selectors, as a basis for stereotypes' (p. 77). Three LEAs were studied which had a larger proportion of women heads than the national average already, and also had 'officers who reported a more favourable attitude to women candidates' (p. 73). If there are women around to provide the selectors with models, or stereotypes, of women heads, more possible styles are available for future candidates to be matched against.

The research team had detailed data on 36 headships being awarded between 1980 and 1983 (table 4.1). Women got appointed in exactly the proportions in which they applied. There are, therefore, some grounds for accepting the complaints that not enough women apply. Morgan *et al.* (1983:67) conclude that the LEA officials went through three phases when considering women candidates for headships:

(1) at the first stage of sifting the applications they welcomed any from women;
(2) at the stage of getting ready to interview they expected women to be of a higher quality than men to make the same shortlist;

Table 4.1 The fate of applicants for thirty-six headships

	Applicants	*Interviewees*	*Appointments*
Total candidates	2,753	96	36
Percentage of women	11	12	11

(3) at the final stages they anticipated hostility from the lay people among the selectors to appointing women to mixed or boys' schools.

Morgan *et al.* (1983) call for more systematic, and job-related, selection procedures, not only to make the appointment of heads more equitable and efficient, but also to allow women a fairer chance.

Sandra Acker (1983) has demolished most of the sociological work on teaching, revealing it to be unscholarly, based on unexamined, circular arguments, and riddled with sexism. The literature on why so few women apply for headships is equally flawed. Researchers, as much as practitioners, make assumptions about the promotion and careers of women teachers which have a basis in staffroom folklore rather than in evidence of any kind. There is a distinct lack of data about men applying for promotion, and particularly about the dynamics of decision making and the financial arrangements in their families, but this has not stopped assumptions being made. The following assumptions are offered as 'explanations' for the small proportion of women teachers reaching promoted posts, especially headships, and have been offered for at least two decades, in that Hilsum and Start (1974) report them from teachers surveyed in 1971, while Davidson (1985) found them among teachers interviewed in 1983.

(1) Men, as breadwinners, need to strive for more money, whereas women, who are only providing 'extra' income, do not.

(2) Men can, and do, expect their families to move house in search of better jobs, which women should not, cannot, or do

not, do.

(3) Men are more persistent in applying for better jobs, and have more self-confidence or ambition, than women.

(4) Men want promotion, women prefer to be classroom teachers rather than do administration.

(5) Women are less well qualified than men.

(6) Women have fewer years of experience than male teachers of the same age.

(7) Women are always leaving to have babies.

(8) Women are more frequently absent from work for inappropriate reasons.

(9) Men are better teachers, and pupils prefer men.

(10) There is discrimination in favour of men, and/or discrimination against women, by heads, appointments committees and the like.

Two kinds of investigation need to be carried out on these beliefs about male and female teachers. First, it would be desirable to discover whether they are true statements about the lives of male and female teachers. Secondly, it would be useful to know how far teachers, heads, advisors, HMIs, education officers, governors and members of local government education committees believe all or any of them to be true and act on them. In the absence of such data we can only treat them as a series of myths or folkbeliefs, which are probably having long-term consequences for the lives of women teachers. If, for example, women teachers believe point 10, they are likely to be discouraged from applying for promotion. Similarly if school governors believe points 1 and 9, they are likely to promote men rather than women.

Our lack of data on the accuracy or falsehood of these statements, and on whether or not they are widely held by educational personnel, is striking. The first nine points, taken together, would form a convincing mythology to hinder the promotion of women in the occupation, and if they are widely believed, evidence to challenge them would have to be extremely powerful and well argued. As a 'mythological charter' for promoting men they could be hard to dislodge. Davidson (1985) presents counter arguments, but they have not reached staffrooms or LEA offices. One possible explanation for women's lower success in reaching higher posts or salaries is that women do not apply. Hilsum and Start (1974) found that in both primary and secondary schools men were promoted faster, and that the number of applications for posts was much higher for men. In a sample of 133 secondary schools that had headships advertised in 1972 there were 4,712 applications from men and only 276 from women. The authors suggest women might not apply because they were convinced they would not get them, but their data show that men apply for posts of a specific status many more times than women. In other words, men who have decided to try for a particular status will persist in applying for such posts, while women do not. Thus male respondents are quoted who made up to 100 applications for a headship, while women respondents who received three or four rejections gave up and stopped applying.

The research by Morgan et al. (1983) a decade later reveals that persistence can be rewarded. They actually observed (pp.62–3) one man eliminated from one shortlist being interviewed and rejected elsewhere, and then gaining a headship in a third school during their research. Another man they came across had made 162 applications for headships before being appointed to a large school. Given the arbitrary and irrational selection procedures that LEAs were using, and there is no reason to suppose that others are different, continued and sustained application is rational. In different LEAs, and in the same LEA at different selection meetings, the same criteria were used positively and negatively. In other words what was a disqualifying factor for one job could be a positive benefit for another. Among the comments recorded by Morgan et al. (1983: 54–62) for and against applicants for headships are the following:

Points made to support a candidate	Points made to attack a candidate
He's had experience in an independent school	Too long in private education

This brief extract from the rich data in Morgan et al. reveals that what one selection group regard as a good quality may be viewed negatively by another – and so anyone wanting promotion should persevere, and persevere, and persevere.

In the 1970s researchers such as Hilsum and Start (1974) claimed that women teachers were less ambitious than men. Subsequent studies have found more ambitious women teachers.

First-class science teacher	and he's a physicist
35 – the right age	A shade on the young side at 34
Got an OU degree	A chap who only passes at the OU hasn't done much
I have a naïve belief in the quality of a first-class honours degree	Don't want anyone with a first because they're too clever to employ
He comes from this part of the world and therefore has sympathy with the kind of children we have to educate	Works in Blanktown and wants to come back to work here – I don't think that's sufficient reason
Good at sport	His interests are squash and drama
Attended my college 6 years after I did	Anyone based at LSE has to be very left in their outlook

The NUT/EOC (1980) research and Davidson (1985) found little difference in the goals of male and female teachers. The women Davidson interviewed were less optimistic that they would reach their goals, but they were ambitious to leave their low-scale jobs for senior positions with administrative duties.

The final two myths – that men are better teachers and that there is sex discrimination in the promotion procedures – are the hardest to gather evidence about. A substantial number of men believe that men make *better* teachers. Given the difficulties of researching such an issue (see Delamont 1986,

1987a) I am not going to discuss it here; it is one of the powerful myths around in British schools.

The question of sex discrimination in promotion, either actual or perceived, is more complex, especially since it was made illegal. The teachers surveyed about coeducation by Dale (1969:48) included women teachers opposed to coeducation because of poorer career opportunities for women. The teachers sampled by Hilsum and Start (1974:15) were asked to rate a list of factors which were thought to influence promotion. About 40 per cent of the 5,794 teachers thought that being a graduate, specialising in a shortage subject, and 'social contacts', were important (respondents could choose up to five factors). 'Being male' was chosen by only 12.8 per cent of the sample. However, among the primary teachers, 16.5 per cent of women but only 6.0 per cent of men thought it important, while among the secondary teachers 20.2 per cent thought being male an advantage. Hilsum and Start followed up the belief that 'social contacts' were important for promotion in their interviews with 135 teachers, and found 75 per cent thought them a significant factor. The kinds of contacts which were mentioned were: Freemason, Church, sports club, political organizations, professional associations, councillor, social club and 'knew the head' (p. 122). It is noticeable that, although the authors do not discuss the point, many of these are male-dominated spheres. Only men can be Freemasons, and far more men are likely to be active in politics, the local council and sports clubs (see Deem (1986) for a discussion on women's participation in voluntary, religious and political activities), and men are in the dominant positions on appointment committees, whether as heads or as LEA staff or local councillors. If the teachers are correct in suggesting that social contacts are important, and it is those kinds of contact which matter, then there are signs of the type of informal male circles which *de facto* exclude women reported for other occupations and professions. Cynthia Epstein (1983) drew attention to the ways in which women in law were excluded from other lawyers' informal circles because these met in bars and clubs closed to women, or at times when women could not attend (see also Atkinson and Delamont 1990, Dale 1987 and Lorber 1984). Hilsum and Start (1974:122) say actual sex discrimination seemed as nebulous as the claims that being promoted meant having the right connections in such organizations as the Freemasons or the Rotary club. They found that there was a 'hearsay grapevine' (p.188) among teachers about such unfair practices, but very few respondents had any direct, personal experience of them.

The study by Morgan *et al.* (1983) found that patronage was a factor in appointments to headships, and that all three groups involved (governors, LEA committee members, and officials) sometimes sponsored particular candidates for reasons to do with non-task matters. In their data there are examples of religious, golfing and party political connections, leading to support for particular applicants. The membership of appointing committees is predominantly male – especially the education officers who have considerable influence over shortlisting – so the authors remark that:

> it is mainly men who are responsible for making decisions about whether women are as capable of being successful headteachers as men. (p.68)

If promotion in school teaching depends in part on meeting heads, councillors and LEA officials at the Freemasons, the rugby club, the Conservative party headquarters, or the golf club, then women are at a considerable disadvantage in school teaching as in other male-dominated professions. The married woman with children has little leisure to be active in politics or sport, as well as manage her job, even if she can enter the relevant premises.

The career in the women's teacher training college has also been changed out of all recognition by the coming of coeducation, and then the closure and merger of colleges. Sheila Fletcher (1984) has chronicled the changes in the Bedford women's PE training college from a cloistered total institution (see Walker 1983) of the type described in *Miss Pym Disposes* (Tey 1947), to a mixed multi-site institute of higher education. There are few studies of those college principals and their careers. Howson (1982) has written a biography of Elizabeth Williams (Principal of Whitelands and Homerton) but we have little information about Williams' coevals or her successors. A whole career avenue for women has been swept away without any public debate, and without any 'rescue archaeology' on the lives of women who chose that career. Browne (1979) has written a history of the Association of Teachers in Colleges and Departments of Education (ATCDE) from 1943 until it was absorbed into NATFHE, and as the ATCDE was formed by amalgamating the Training College Association (founded 1891) and the Council of Principals (1913), her book includes data on women college principals this century. Women were in a majority in the Council of Principals, and between the wars there was an abortive move by a few men to form a separate association to escape a perceived female dominance (p.9). In the period 1918–39, lecturing in a college of education, though a respectable occupation for women, was not a highly paid one, for the salaries were the same as those for teaching in elementary school (p.26). Even the principals did not receive generous salaries, because until 1965 there was no agreed, national salary scale for them. As Browne comments wryly:

> before that the salaries were based on gentlemen's agreements in each college. As the majority of the gentlemen on the principals' side were ladies, they did not do very well. (p.134)

Lecturing in a teachers' training college, or being principal of one, was not a well-paid occupation, but it was a career, and gave women autonomy. In 1957 there were 108 two year teacher training colleges: nineteen for men, fifteen mixed, and seventy-four for women only. Many of these had women principals. However, after 1944 the criticisms of single-sex colleges grew in strength, so that gradually they became to be seen as anachronisms. In 1969 one retiring principal of a women's college told Browne that her generation were the 'last of the lay abbesses' (p. 134). They were, and a whole career path went with them.

Thus, in 30 years two career paths for women were lost, and nothing was done to replace them with alternatives in the new coeducational schools and multi-course tertiary colleges. Similar analyses can be made for nursing, librarianship and social work, where reorganization and bureaucratization have led to senior posts increasingly being held by men. As Heath (1981) pointed out:

school-teaching, nursing and social work ... the helping professions provide a definite channel of upward mobility for career-orientated women. (p.120)

If the senior posts in these occupations are becoming monopolized by men, then women will be trapped in the lower-paid grades of these occupations with little chance of promotion. The sociology of education and professional socialization has not yet begun to focus on the consequences of this for these occupations, for social mobility, for women's lives and careers, and for the ways these workers handle male and female clients.

As far as pupils are concerned, the lack of women in top educational jobs is glaringly obvious. Eileen Byrne (1978:212) sees the resulting absence of women in leadership roles as disadvantageous to males and females. She argues that:

> It is crucial that both girls and boys actually *see* women in leadership, management, government, making decisions in their daily lives, if we are to break the cycle of under-achievement. As long as children see men taking the top posts, decisions, and higher pay, ... children will believe what they see and not what we say ...

Byrne wants to see 'both men and women evenly represented at all stages from pre-school to professors, primaries to polytechnics ...' (p. 213). The evidence we have shows that this is far from being achieved. However, even if Byrne's ideal balance of the sexes were achieved, the evidence on recruitment to teaching and the 'reality shock' which hits recruits suggest that it would need more than an equal balance of the sexes to change the sexist nature of the occupational culture. There are strong historical reasons for the occupational culture of teachers being a conservative one where sex roles are concerned.

5 Strategies for change

> Sichelgaita was cast in a Wagnerian mould and must be appreciated as such. In her we came face to face with the closest approximation history has ever dared to produce of a Valkyrie. A woman of immense build and colossal physical strength, she was to prove a perfect wife for Robert, and from the day of their wedding to that of his death she scarcely ever left her husband's side – least of all in battle, one of her favourite occupations.
>
> (Norwich 1967:117)

Sichelgaita married Robert (the Norman ruler of Apulia) in 1058 or 1059 and bore him ten children as well as riding into battle with him. We know about her partly from the writing of Anna Comnena, daughter of the Byzantine emperor Alexius, 'an intelligent and very well-educated woman; and she was a conscientious historian, who tried to verify her sources' (Runciman 1951:327). The majority of British schoolchildren and students have never heard of either woman, and leave formal education without realizing that any female wrote chronicles about wars or (other than Boudicca) ever fought in battle.

Sichelgaita and Anna Comnena may seem remote from the history that contemporary British pupils need to know. Yet British undergraduates are equally ignorant of women such as Mary Seacole (the black nurse who served heroically in the Crimea) and Prudence Crandall (who was firebombed out of Connecticut towns for trying to teach negroes to read), whose existence and exploits are bursting with contemporary relevance. The funny book by Kate Charlesworth and Marsaili Cameron (1986) written because most British histories include 'about 3½ women', including Boudicca, is designed to redress the male bias of the history curriculum. In this chapter the focus is attempts made at national, local, school and individual level to change the ways in which schools have reinforced conventional sex roles (cultural reproduction) rather than challenging them (cultural interruption).

Since the first edition of this book there have been a good many projects designed to reduce sex stereotyping in education. In a book this short there is no room to discuss all of these, so the chapter takes one such initiative – Women's Training Roadshows – examines it, and then draws some conclusions about all the attempts.

One initiative discussed

In June 1987 over 2,000 female pupils, mostly between 12 and 18, visited the Cardiff Women's Training Roadshow, an exhibition, filmshow, careers convention and workshop designed to widen their horizons about non-traditional jobs (Pilcher *et al.* 1988, 1989a, b). This was the eighth in a series of such events held round Britain run by the Women's National Commission between 1985 and 1987. Roadshows are unusual compared to most of the other programmes designed to challenge sex-role stereotyping in education because they were a *national* initiative. Venues included Cardiff and Glasgow. The Cardiff Roadshow was the only one to be evaluated, and the researchers' conclusions are a useful starting point for thinking about initiatives since 1980. The full results have been published (Pilcher *et al.* 1989a, c) so the issues raised here are brief and selective. Overall the Roadshow was a great success for sponsors, exhibitors, participants and visitors. However, the benefits were unevenly spread in the locality and among the schoolgirls who visited it.

A Roadshow costs a good deal of money (raised from industry, commerce and government agencies) and involves many people in a vast amount of work. For a school, visiting a Roadshow is a cheap and easy way to do something about sex equality, because the costs fall elsewhere. All the secondary schools with female pupils in three local authorities in South Wales were invited to send parties of pupils and teachers to the Roadshow. Many did not even reply to the invitation, which indicates how little importance most heads attach to female careers' advice and equal opportunities. There are, for example, four Welsh-medium secondary schools in the area, but only one accepted the invitation. A few schools were enthusiastic and sent large numbers of girls, but many others were uninterested in the opportunity.

There were also noticeable differences among those schools which did send pupils in the amount of preparation for the visit that had been done, the plans made about what pupils would do there, and hence the benefits for staff and schoolgirls. For example, the adolescents were given an activity booklet to structure their use of the Roadshow (schools had been told about this in the precirculated materials), yet almost all schools allowed the young women to come without pens or pencils! In following one pair of young women as they ambled around the exhibition hall (who had drifted past most of the stalls without engaging in conversation with the staff or taking part in activities) this lack of preparation in their school was apparent to me. When they went to the area containing role models (real live women who were bus drivers, engineers, dentists and carpenters), the girls appeared to be unaware of the purpose of this part of the Roadshow. I intervened, saying 'Have you found a role model to talk to?' and steered them to the veterinary nurses. One girl commented 'We haven't been told anything about this', and followed up a talk with the veterinary nurses by speaking to the women bus driver and inspector. They had had *no idea* of the active part they were supposed to be playing.

Few staff used the exhibition *themselves* to collect materials or talk to employers and role models: the typical teacher made sure all the pupils got off the bus and into the building and then vanished until it was time to leave. Exhibitors and role models both said afterwards that the pupils had not been properly prepared to gain from the event: they did not know what to ask about or look for. Pupils reported later that many of the exhibitors and role models were not keen to talk to schoolgirls, but were self-absorbed. Orian McGann (1987) wrote:

presentation varied considerably between displays, on the one hand some participants showed enthusiasm and attempted to attract students to their stands, on the other hand, however, a number of those observed seemed to be doing the opposite and I got the feeling these presenters were *hoping* that they wouldn't be approached! (p.7)

McGann found that people staffing the stalls were not necessarily volunteers and/or interested in promoting sex equality at all. For some, it was just a job. As Guttentag and Bray (1976) showed, half-hearted attempts to challenge sex roles are *not* even half-effective: attempts that are poorly done or done by non-believers tend to reinforce conservatism in pupils.

As a 15 year old complained:

Some stalls were only there to advertise and not to speak to the girls.

The research on the VISTA (women scientists and technologists visiting schools to explain their jobs) element of the Girls into Science and Technology (GIST) project (Whyte 1985) makes it very clear that the role models only work if they are properly prepared and briefed, and the 'lessons' to be learnt by pupils are made explicit.

Of the 2,000 schoolgirls who had attended the Roadshow 500 were subsequently visited at their schools and asked about their responses to it. There was a wide range of attitudes according to the young women's ages and the type of school attended. A sixth former at a private school who had been exposed to WISE (Women into Science and Engineering Year), been on a work-shadowing programme, done three sciences to O-level and planned to be a doctor told us almost wearily:

Being at this school, everyone is told that they can do anything. We have had it all.

In contrast, younger pupils – those of 12, 13 and 14 – were surprised to discover that women 'were allowed' to be plumbers, bus drivers and solicitors. As one said

It was very interesting. I didn't think there was so many jobs available to women.

One of the role models, a chemical engineer, reported two younger women asked her three times if she was 'really an engineer'. She enquired why they doubted her, to get the answer 'because you've got a handbag'. These pupils were still at primary school in 1984 – WISE Year – and held precisely the attitudes that it was designed to change. One lesson from this is that all these initiatives have to be done for every generation of women: the first-year pupils do not 'know' what the fifth form were taught about sex roles 4 years earlier.

One of the striking findings of this evaluation was the young women's surprise that important national companies – such as BP – thought they were worth putting on an exhibition for. Many of the schoolgirls were flattered that firms thought they justified such effort and expense.

The Women's Training Roadshow aimed to give girls and women information about the opportunities available to them in non-traditional female occupations. The general message of the Roadshow did get over to its audience – perhaps especially so to the younger pupils who enjoyed their involvement in the participatory activities. Each schoolgirl's visit to the Roadshow lasted less than 3 hours. The follow-up visits to the schools took place some 4 months after that. The impact that made on the girls can be judged by their recall of the event, which was detailed and vivid, and by the level of support for future events. Our analysis of the girls' attitudes towards women and work and issues of childcare reveal that they generally hold egalitarian and non-stereotyped views. Yet, however egalitarian and non-stereotyped the views of the girls might be, this does not mean that they are considering attempting non-traditional occupations themselves. The occupational aspirations of the majority of the schoolgirls are safely within the well-established realms of 'women's work', and they were not doing physics and CDT after 14 (see Pratt *et al.* 1984).

The girls in our study maintained that their decisions about which subjects to study to examination level were made on the basis of their interest and ability and whether a subject would be useful for a job that they had in mind. However, from comments that were made in the discussion sessions in relation to physics and other non-traditional subjects, it is clear that a 'hidden agenda' is in operation involving their perception of the subject matter and their consequent ability to do well in it. The girls described physics as a subject which was 'boring' and 'hard'. They explained that boys are less likely to view the subject in this way because the subject matter, as the girls perceived it, is more likely to appeal to them. A sixth former, from a private school, told us: 'Boys are encouraged in these things from an early age with toys'.

Many girls also believed that physics teachers, who were invariably male, had a negative attitude towards girls, who were most often a minority in their classes. It was explained to us frequently that physics is a subject which 'leads to male careers' and that this is a further reason why girls choose not to study it. The 'hidden agenda' in relation to physics thus involves the girls' perception of the subject matter and their ideas about its occupational implications. It is the subject matter of physics, or, more probably, the way it is presented, that needs to be addressed if the numbers of girls choosing to study the subject are to increase.

We asked about the girls' own plans and hopes, both expected and desired destinations after leaving school. There is a large literature both international (Kuvlesky and Bealer 1972) and local (Cowell *et al.* 1981) showing that adolescents separate their ideal jobs from their occupational expectations which are more conditioned by local labour market conditions. Table 5.1 shows what the pupils hoped and expected to do after leaving school. The sample included a wide range of abilities yet a large proportion of the girls (35 per cent) hope to go to university after they leave school; 30 per cent of the schoolgirls hope to get a full-time job whilst just over 20 per cent hope to train in a college. A comparison of their expectations for the future rather than their hopes is revealing.

Aspirations to attend university and to get a full-time job are greater than expectations. Getting a place on a Youth Training Scheme, getting a part-time job or training in a college are expected more frequently than desired. An examination of the explanations for the gap between their expectations and their hopes reveals a concern about the young women's ability to gain appropriate qualifications (59 per cent) and unemployment (19

Table 5.1 Hoped for and expected destinations after leaving school

Destination	Hope Number	%	Expected Number	%	Differential %
University or Polytechnic	173	35	144	30	−5
Full-time job	150	30	81	17	−14
Training in a college	107	22	110	23	+1
Studying GCE	58	12	57	12	0
Part-time job	22	4	46	10	+6
Start a family	14	3	16	3	0
YTS	12	2	30	6	+4
Help at home	4	1	9	2	+1
Don't know	8	2	46	10	+8
Other	17	3	14	3	0

Percentages do not add up to 100 because of some respondents naming more than one destination.

per cent). Other explanations include changing their minds (11 per cent), financial concerns (4 per cent), the responsibilities of marriage and family life (4 per cent) and that achievement of aspirations requires determination (4 per cent). It is clear that the girls view barriers to achievement of aspirations in personal and individual terms, expressed as failure to obtain appropriate levels and types of qualifications, or a lack of determination or conviction on their own part. Societal or structural barriers are mentioned less.

Most of the young women wanted secretarial jobs (10 per cent), or to enter nursery nursing (10 per cent), hairdressing and beauty (10 per cent) or teaching (9 per cent); 6 per cent of the sample wanted to be 'lawyers' or 'solicitors'; and smaller percentages chose medicine, dentistry, veterinary science, and accountancy. Very few girls aspired to non-traditional manual occupations, such as plumbing. Only 1 per cent of the sample favoured engineering for themselves. Overall, the girls were aiming to enter occupational areas which are safely 'female', with a minority aiming for 'professional' occupations, such as law and medicine.

The main effect of the Roadshow, and any other sex-equality information the young women had received in the past, was to make them aware that women *could* do non-traditional jobs, *not* to change their own preferences for traditional female ones or the professions of law and medicine.

An initiative such as the Roadshow provides a wealth of data, far more than can be discussed here (see Pilcher *et al.* 1989a, c). Action-research programmes that last for longer periods – such as Girls into Science and Technology (GIST) which ran for 2 years – generate enough material to fill whole books. It would be foolhardy, and boring for the reader, to present a compressed finding of all the projects that have run since 1980. Instead, I have extracted some key issues from the Roadshow evaluation which are also applicable to other studies, and used them to raise the central topics which need to be thought about for the 1990s.

Since 1980: what have we learnt?

The Roadshow has many features in common with other national and local attempts to reduce sex differentiation and stereotyping in education. If the next decades' efforts are to be consolidated and extended there are four groups of features from which lessons can be learnt: locational, directional, 'vocational'/'cultural', and psychological.

The locational issues are that Roadshows and other initiatives are:

(a) concentrated in England rather than Wales, Scotland and Ireland;
(b) in urban rather than rural settings.

The directional issues are that Roadshows and other initiatives are:

(a) aimed at girls and women not boys and men;
(b) directed to secondary and tertiary sector students not nursery, infant and primary school pupils;
(c) aimed at school pupils rather than parents, trade unions, employers and teachers.

The 'vocational'/'cultural' issues are that Roadshows and other such initiatives are:

(a) focused on science and CDT, not humanities and aesthetic subjects;
(b) based on an assumption that schools and workplaces are sites for labour, not primarily places for socializing;
(c) concentrated on the serious rather than the pleasurable.

The psychological issues are that Roadshows and other initiatives are:

(a) focused on what adults believe will change pupils' ideas, rather than starting from what pupils actually believe (their 'folk models');
(b) sanitized to avoid all discussion of sexuality, orientation and sexual politics.

These are explained as they are discussed below.

Lost horizons? The location of initiatives

The Women's National Commission Roadshows were held around Britain not just in England. Most of the initiatives which have taken place since the first edition of this book have been English and localized in a few LEAs. Burchell and Millman's (1989) useful collection on projects and policies being implemented to bring about gender equality has nothing from Northern Ireland, Scotland or Wales; neither do the volumes in the same series by Weiner (1985) and Wickham (1985).

The Weiner volume is particularly narrow in its geographical coverage: twelve of the seventeen contributors work in London, none north of Leeds, and all in cities. All the Roadshows were held in urban areas, and this pattern is typical of most sex-equality projects. Clwyd County Council's appointment of a sex-equality advisor, and their translation of *Genderwatch* into Welsh, are a rare example of a rural initiative. Taylor (1980) has pointed out how the government reports on the Scottish secondary curriculum in the 1970s ignored sex inequalities completely, and how male dominated the administration of Scottish education was. Too much of the effort to make schools less sex stereotyped has been concentrated in a few English cities. Only the national data which are collected to evaluate the national programmes such as TVEI will reveal whether all LEAs are working equally hard to reduce sex differentiation. Byrne (1978) claimed that girls in rural areas suffered more than those in towns from sex differentiation, so the impact of initiatives throughout the whole UK is particularly important.

TVEI, which started in England and Wales in a small way in 1983, reached Scotland in 1984, and now covers 100 LEAs. In Scotland, TVEI had become widespread by 1987 (Bell and Howieson 1988). Nationally, local authorities signing up for TVEI have to accept the criterion that:

> equal opportunities should be available to young people of both sexes and they should normally be educated together on courses within each project. Care should be taken to avoid sex-stereotyping.

> (MSC 1984)

It is not clear that this is recognized at school and classroom level. In South Wales, the TVEI course at Brynhenlog involved boys doing 'keyboard skills' in one room, while girls did 'typing' in another, *not* because either sex would benefit from being in a single-sex class but because typing used to be a 'girls' subject, and the TVEI 'keyboard skills' had just been added for boys (see Upton *et al.* (1988) and Delamont 1989a for details of this research). Away from the self-consciously anti-sexist schools in some LEAs, such reinterpretations of TVEI are probably all too common.

As well as being geographically restricted, most initiatives have left out one sex altogether.

Lost boys? The directional issue

The Cardiff Women's Training Roadshow, and the others in the WNC series, were for females. Schools were asked to send parties of girls, and the publicity was aimed at women. The stallholders, role models and workshops were designed to challenge women's ideas about the labour market. This is typical of the majority of initiatives designed to change the sexual division of labour in Britain. Few projects have been aimed at discovering why boys avoid foreign languages and home economics, choose 'masculine' jobs and plan to stay in the labour market rather than stay home to rear their children. The research that has been done receives less publicity, and generates less concern, than that on girls. Powell (Powell 1979, 1984, 1986, Powell and Littlewood 1982, 1983) has been voicing concern for a decade about the small numbers of boys gaining a foreign language qualification, but there has not been a single project like GIST aimed at boys. Noticeably, Powell's research is not even cited in the Burchell and Millman (1989) collection, or that on boys edited by Askew and Ross (1988). In 1973 only 8 per cent of male sixth formers in English LEA schools were taking A-level French compared to 24 per cent of girls. Yet nowhere in the DES documents produced in the 1970s was this raised as a problem. While the shortage of female scientists and technologists has generated research and action, the shortage of male linguists has been ignored. No one has suggested that all soldiers stationed in Germany should seize the chance to learn German, or those in Cyprus be taught Greek, yet these are wasted opportunities to reach young men.

The wider issues of gender and science are being debated in the 1980s as never before, predominantly by women authors (e.g. Rossiter 1982, Manthorpe 1982, Burrage 1983, Keller 1985, J. Harding 1986, S. Harding 1986, Harding and O'Barr 1987, Doherty 1987, McNeill 1988). Debates about the extent to which scientific activity is inherently an aggressive combative activity are pursued in feminist scholarship, although they were not taken up in sociology of science or science education. Alison Kelly (1985a) presented this debate to the sociology of education audience, and Manthorpe (1982) raised it for science educators, but it has not been rehearsed in the journals read by historians and sociologists of science (Delamont 1987b; 1989c). Despite that neglect, the general level of interest is massive compared to the silence on men and languages. The problem remains acute. Jones (1989) presents the A-level entry figures for Wales by sex comparing 1967, 1977 and 1987. In 1987 women were 23 per cent of all the A-level physics candidates and 83 per cent of all the French entrants. The English statistics are similar. In Europe men expect to learn other languages whatever career they plan to enter, yet in the UK they do not, and studying languages may even be seen as 'sissy'. A series of Roadshows for schoolboys on the need for fluency in many tongues, and a FLAMES (Foreign Languages are Men's Subjects) programme are clearly called for.

This particular sex differentiation may be changed by the introduction of the 'National' (national here meaning only England and Wales) Curriculum. It is too soon to say how the National Curriculum will work out in practice. Those commentators who were alarmed by the small percentage of women doing any science after 16 and the shortage of females studying physics after 14 welcomed the compulsory science (although it is not clear whether there will be enough teachers to instruct them). Initial enthusiasm for the central place for science became suspicion when the 'two tier' science curriculum was proposed. Research on how pupils are allocated to particular subjects (e.g. Woods 1979) is currently of crucial importance in science education given the proposal that some pupils should have only 12.5 per cent of their time occupied by science, rather than 20 per cent. Edwyn Jones (1988), then chairperson elect of the ASE (Association for Science Education), rightly enquired who would decide which pupils received the 12.5 per cent. He feared that girls, or the brightest arts specialists, or the less able, might be allowed to take the reduced provision. Anyone who has read Keddie (1971) might fear that unexamined teacher assumptions about 'natural' talent will be used to allocate pupils to the 12.5 per cent 'stream'. Research into the possible existence of processes and policies that Keddie (1971) claimed to have found in humanities is needed among science, maths and CDT staff.

The focus on female pupils rather than males is not the only directional issue that needs comment. Many employers still do not have any interest in recruiting, training and retaining workers in non-traditional occupations; many trade unions have yet to take sex equality on board at a workplace, everyday level; and many parents, teachers and even careers staff have very stereotyped ideas about male and female behaviour. Roadshows were sponsored by major national firms, and some local ones also supported the Cardiff one. Many other employers showed no interest. The local commercial television station (HTV) did not reply to the invitation to join the Roadshow, yet the training officer visited it and complained that she had not been asked to participate because HTV were keen to recruit women as technicians. We explained that HTV had not answered the invitation they had been sent – which had never reached the training officers. It is inconceivable that an offer of a Royal Visit or a trip to the Cup Final could get lost in a British firm, but all too easy to believe that a letter offering a Roadshow stall would. Rees *et al.* (1989) report that many employers in South Wales, studied in 1986 and 1987, held

> stereotyped beliefs about differences in the technical and social abilities of men and women . . . (and) such stereotypes were further consolidated by cultural assumptions about the gender-appropriateness of different jobs – and where men or women . . . entered 'inappropriate' jobs, it was often the employer who guided them away . . . into other work.

Encouraging young people into non-traditional occupations is pointless if their employers are going to redirect them away from those jobs. Cockburn (1987) has shown vividly how hard it is for an adolescent who chooses an unconventional job to sustain it under pressures from adults and peers.

Projects and initiatives designed to challenge sex stereotyping have to be aimed at males and females, employers and workers, teachers and taught, parents and children, advisors and advised. If they are not, the initiative suffers the Lake Wobegon effect. Lake Wobegon, Mist County, Minnesota, does not appear on any map of the USA. As Garrison Keiller (1986:90–2) explains, four teams of surveyors began from the four corners of Minnesota, working towards the centre:

> The southwest and northwest contingents moved fast over level ground, while the eastern teams got bogged down in the woods, so that when they met a little west of Lake Wobegon, the four quadrants didn't fit within the boundaries legislated by Congress in 1851. . . . The legislature simply re-proportioned the state by eliminating the overlap in the middle, the little quadrangle that is Mist County.
>
> Ever since 1866, therefore, Lake Wobegon has not been on any map.

Educational reforms tend to vanish in the same way. Gillian Parsons (1981) found this when researching how teachers, university lecturers and public examiners felt about the choice of O- and A-level set texts for English literature. She interviewed heads of English in comprehensives, who told her that the choice of texts was dull and predictable, and they wished that the universities and the examiners would be more adventurous. The representatives of the exam boards reported that the choice of texts for O- and A-levels was dull and predictable, but that neither the schools nor the universities were prepared to accept more adventurous selections. Staff in the universities told Parsons that the choice of texts was dull and predictable but the exam boards and schools were not prepared to accept more adventurous selections. Literature by women, from the Commonwealth, and Anglo-Welsh texts were all excluded from the lists year after year; while all three sets of participants agreed the status quo was dull, yet blamed the other two groups for blocking innovation.

The same Lake Wobegon effect occurs in the area of reducing sex stereotyping. Teachers blame parents, pupils and the labour market; parents blame schools, pupils and employers; employers blame schools, parents and young people; young people complain about adults. No group admits that they can change the status quo, and the educational equivalent of Mist County (sex equality) stays missing from the centre of the map.

Science or sculpture? The vocational/cultural issues

The musical *Salad Days* featured a magic piano which made everyone who heard it start dancing, even a killjoy cabinet minister. The initiatives designed to reduce sex segregation and differentiation desperately need such an instrument. The programmes and innovations have been serious, prosaic and leaden footed: Apollonian not Dionysian. There has been very little joy, gaiety and dancing. The thrust of the initiatives has been towards science and technology, towards vocational subjects, and towards the intrinsic rewards of work. Very little has been done about sex equality in the humanities and the aesthetic curriculum, in leisure activities, as a way of having a more pleasurable life, and to the social and emotional aspects of working. There are no programmes designed to enthuse girls with the ambition to be poets or sculptors, to get boys enjoying ballet or *petit point*, or to encourage the sexes to practice working together and sharing hobbies and recreational chatter. Tickle's (1987) collection on the arts in education does not include a single report (in eleven chapters) of any initiative to challenge sexism in these areas. There is a desperate need for projects that focus on all areas of the curriculum, and those which stress that liberation from rigid sex roles makes life fun for both sexes. The schoolchildren studied by Raphaela Best (1983) were quite clear at 15 that:

> they could do and say what they wanted, they were indeed egalitarian, they were indeed non-sexist, they could indeed relate to one another on the basis of common interests – as friends – without resorting to macho aggression or female wiles. (p.178)

Elaine told an interviewer 'we had a fun time' in Best's anti-sexism programme. Such fun is too often missing.

The lack of gaiety in the programmes to reduce sex differentiation in education is closely related to a second characteristic they share. Initiatives are heavily biased towards the view that life in schools, further education colleges, and workplaces is centred on the work that goes on there, which should be intrinsically satisfying. This is contrary to the experience of most pupils in their schools and at their part-time jobs, and to research on workers; it therefore makes the emphasis of the programmes seem irrelevant and rarefied.

There is ample evidence that many pupils value school as much or more for the social life – seeing friends and catching up on news – as they do for the lessons or eventual qualifications. As a Scottish school leaver put it:

> Once I left school I thought it was great, then you miss all of your pals, you miss all of the laughs.

> (Walford 1989:260)

Margaret Gibson's (1987a,b) research on Punjabi high school

students in Northern California reports that they are deviant because they concentrate on academic work even when they are not in the college-preparatory track. The local 'Anglo' students outside the college track do the minimum necessary to get a high school graduation certification:

> There is an assumption, shared by Valleysider parents, students, and teachers, that the more advanced academic courses are only for college-bound students. Those students who do not expect to go on to a 4-year college see little point, therefore, in taking maths, science, and English classes beyond those required for graduation. . . . Thus for the last 2 years of high school, the typical Valleysider student turns his or her attention to part 'time jobs and social activities.
> (Gibson 1987b:307)

The Punjabi students were seen as deviant failures because they did not join in school clubs, dances, class picnics, etc. They are viewed as unassimilated because they take schoolwork seriously.

In the labour market, the same criteria apply. Carol Buswell's (1988) study of fifty-five adolescents in YTS placements in clerical and retail workplaces reveals how important for the trainees the social relations were. The intrinsic nature of the work was dull and repetitive, but a good placement resulted from friendly, supportive colleagues. Buswell (1988:170) quotes a girl on a clerical placement whose workmates 'invited me to the dinner-dance and paid for me and everything', while one in a shop said hers were 'very helpful and nice' and treated her 'like an equal'. Most of the research on the types of work that the majority of the population does shows it to be undemanding, uninteresting and repetitive. (See, for example, Blackburn and Mann 1979, and Pollert 1981.)

Blackburn and Mann pointed out that most of the men they studied used more skill when driving *to work* than they needed to perform their tasks at work. It is the social relationships that differentiate good and bad jobs, and the lack of them is one reason why unemployment is so depressing (see Coffield *et al.* 1986; Walford 1989). Few people are privileged to have jobs that are intrinsically absorbing or satisfying. A major problem for young people who try to enter non-traditional jobs is the lack of supportive, enjoyable friendships in the workplace. (See Cockburn (1987), for example, where this lack affects both boys and girls on YTS.) Too much of the effort put into reducing sex differentiation is based on a model of working life where intrinsic satisfaction is enough, ignoring the realities of the jobs young people actually face. It is no use persuading a girl to get an apprenticeship in a garage if none of the men is able to be workmates with a female.

Advice about choosing non-traditional occupations will be 'written off' if it is offered in careers lessons riddled with misapprehensions about the world of work the adolescents already know. In 1985 I watched a careers lesson for remedial and mildly learning-disabled pupils in a Welsh comprehensive school, Heol-y-Crynwyr, taken by the Deputy Head, Mr Despenser.

> The lesson is centred round a book about starting work. Frank starts his first job, and does everything wrong: he is late, he hasn't brought his NI card, etc., he is cheeky and does not radiate keenness etc.
>
> His boss is angry with him. The pupils read the story aloud and then discuss it. They all side with Frank, and regard the boss as quite unreasonable for shouting at him.
>
> Mr Despenser tries to refocus them onto their responsibilities, such as punctuality and politeness. He asks for their ideas on what happens when a young person starts work, and then disputes all their ideas. Frederick said the worst thing about starting work was that it would 'Be a new place, wouldn't know nobody there'.
>
> Mr Despenser said that was irrelevant, and asked what time a shopworker has to start work in the morning.
>
> Claudette said '7.00', and Mr Despenser told her that was too early, shops did not open that early in the morning. She tried to tell him about shops that do, but he ignored her.

The shop at the end of the road outside the school, a newsagent and general store, announced on its door that it was open from 7.00 a.m. to 7.00 p.m. Too many of the initiatives fail to use the knowledge pupils have and face the realities they face.

Whose heads are we in? The 'psychological' dimension

At first glance school physics, smoking in pregnancy, a proper
roast dinner and Basque cheesemaking have nothing in common
with each other, and no place in a book on sex roles and the
school. In fact all those topics have been the focus of research on
how ordinary people think about the world around them and
the everyday things in it. Experts frequently despair because
people do not follow good advice or behave in self-damaging
ways or fail to learn what they are taught. Doctors, nurses and
midwives, for example, are distressed when mothers smoke,
drink and take tranquillizers even in pregnancy. In a range of
areas, researchers have decided to start at the other end of the
problem: to find out how ordinary lay people understand their
everyday worlds, and then compare their 'lay' or 'folk' models
with those held by experts. Frequently, it transpires that the
people in the street have a clear logically consistent folk model
which is quite, quite different from 'scientific' or 'expert'
models. When a folk model conflicts with expert argument, the
former usually wins out: because it was developed over a
person's lifetime, in their home, school, job and family setting,
and works there, it is more powerful than the abstract 'theories'
of outsiders.

A concrete example from the area of food and eating will
illustrate this. Anne Murcott (1983, 1988) studied the folk
models of food and nutrition held by women in South Wales.
Although her respondents had learnt about vitamins, minerals
and protein in school, and could describe food in those terms, it
was not the model they used when planning menus, shopping
and cooking. When actually getting food on to the table, the
model used was one of 'meals and platefuls'. For example,
everyone had an idea of 'a cooked dinner' or 'a proper dinner',
consisting of roast meat, roast and boiled potatoes, a green
vegetable and another vegetable, plus gravy. This was con-
trasted with snacks, salad meals, chip-based meals, curries,
Chinese take-aways and so on. When organizing their family's
food, the lay model of types of meal, plus the likes and dislikes
of family members, plus the constraints of time, money,
availability and, importantly, the views of the husband, gov-

erned what was cooked and eaten. The dietitians' model, though known, was not relevant compared to the folk model of what a good wife put on the table in front of her family.

Exactly the same findings come from science education. Even people who have done A-level sciences still have 'folk models' or 'misapprehensions' about how scientific phenomena (such as gravity) work. If you ask 15 year olds a science question framed like a school science task, they use their school science to answer it. If they are asked a question needing the same scientific information to answer it, but phrased like an everyday enquiry, commonsense lay models are invoked. So, for example, the same pupils who can answer a science question about expansion of heated metals correctly, fail to explain why sausages burst their skins when cooked. The scientific information does not displace the folk model, it merely sits in a compartment alongside it. The research on this topic (e.g. Driver 1983, Gilbert and Watts 1983) is mostly read within science education, but there are implications beyond that. Aggleton *et al.* (1988, 1989) have shown how adolescents' understanding of AIDS is based in folk biology which often conflicts with official health education information. Some of the folk models about biological phenomena are undiluted descendants from the ideas of Aristotle: the Basque shepherds studied by Ott (1986) for example still have Aristotle's theory of conception.

Many people reject, or compartmentalize, scientific theory, because it conflicts with their deeply embedded folk models. People also balance information from each model they have, which explains why people 'damage' their own health. Mothers knew smoking was bad for them, but also knew if they did not smoke their families suffered because they were tense and stressed. Relaxing by smoking led to benefits for the health and welfare of the rest of the household.

The consequences of accepting that pupils have their own folk models of how the world works for designing teaching are potentially far reaching. In school science the proponents of the misapprehensions approach want teachers to discover what pupils' folk models of, for example, weight, mass and density, are, and then design a series of experiments to demonstrate that the folk model is not sufficiently robust or universal to explain all phenomena relating to weight, mass and density. Pupils would recapitulate parts of the history of science as they moved from their models to scientific truth which *would* displace the folk originals. Measor (1989) has argued the same point in relation to sex education, although she does not refer to the science education authors at all.

The lessons for initiatives designed to change sex roles in schools are clear. First, it is important that such programmes start from the target group's current lay beliefs about science, or CDT, or sex roles, or engineering, or childrearing. Most of the initiatives that have been tried in Britain have ignored the ideas that teachers and/or pupils may have in their heads already. If teachers believe that sex roles are genetically determined (women are naturally more patient with small children), or pupils that any adolescent girl who takes an apprenticeship in a garage is 'boy mad' and any boy interested in fashion design is gay, programmes to change their ideas and practices have to start from those premises.

Conclusions

The attempts to challenge sexism in education, and to raise the aspirations of female pupils, have been enormously successful given the small numbers of enthusiasts and low levels of funding available. The criticisms given in this chapter stem from a desire to see the next wave of programmes reach further and be more successful. The shortage of school leavers in the next few years is a golden opportunity for young people of both sexes to choose jobs that suit them untrammelled by sexist prejudices, and the schools will need to prepare them for that world.

6 Conclusion:
the way forward

How do I feel about walking two steps behind a black man?
Side by side, baby, or nobody walks at all.
(Terry Babb, a black woman graduate student at Columbia,
talking in Harrison 1973:109)

Terry Babb is describing the complex relationships of black
American men and women, where issues of race, class and
gender are inextricably linked. Her comment will, however,
serve very well as the motto for this final chapter. There are
three sections in the chapter: on the future for research, for
schools, pupils and teachers, and for the whole education
system.

The future for research

There are three issues which need to be addressed here:
'feminist research', the agenda of necessary research, and the
dissemination of those findings. Since the first edition of this
book there has been a rapid growth of studies conducted with
feminist methods and discussions of what such methods might
be (e.g. Roberts 1981, Stanley and Wise 1983, Bowles and Duelli
Klein 1983, Butler 1984, Roberts 1984, Harding 1987). Clegg
(1985) is an excellent summary of the claims for and against
feminist methods, and Eichler (1988) is a practical handbook for
doing non-sexist research. This book is not an appropriate place
to examine all the arguments (see Delamont 1991), but a brief
excursion into the debate is necessary.

At the end of J. E. Flecker's play *Hassan* (1922:169) the 'great
summer caravan for the cities of the Far North East'

(Samarkand and Bokhara) leaves Baghdad. It is an all-male affair, made up of merchants, pilgrims and camel drivers, who march out of the city singing joyfully. The women of Baghdad argue and plead that the men should stay at home, complaining that:

> They have their dreams, and do not think of us

while the gatekeeper comments:

> What would ye, ladies? It was ever thus,
> Men are unwise and curiously planned.

The wave of enthusiasm for feminist methodology in the last decade among some male and female scholars presumably stems from a desire to integrate the golden journey, and discover what *women's* dreams are. The debates over the theory and practice of feminist research seem to have left educational research untouched, just as they have yet to appear in some of the methods textbooks. The third edition of Cohen and Manion's (1989) otherwise excellent book of educational research techniques does not contain any discussion of, or reference to, feminist methods, or even any consideration of non-sexist approaches to research.

There are several different arguments put forward about what feminist methods are. One line of thought is that feminists should only use qualitative methods, because quantitative ones are part of a patriarchal pseudo-scientific 'malestream' culture. Arguing that quantitative methods are unsuitable or unacceptable for feminist research insults researchers who use them; ignores the fact that policy makers are often more influenced by numbers than accounts; and makes unduly optimistic assumptions about qualitative research. (The first two arguments can be followed up in Jayaratne (1983), the last in Lofland (1971).)

The argument should not be about whether to use quantitative or qualitative methods, but about how to use methods reflexively (Hammersley and Atkinson 1983). That is, to be self-conscious about the whole research process, and to use research to make the familiar problematic. Feminist methods are fine if 'feminism' does not become another unexamined, taken-for-granted perspective on the world rather than a lens for making that world unfamiliar. This argument is made eloquently by Stanley and Wise (1983) and permeates Dorothy Smith's (1987) work, and there is no space to elaborate it here. Readers who want a clear guideline on how to do non-sexist research should consult Eichler (1988:11) who offers robust commonsense:

> a study may be entirely non-sexist and still be trivial or otherwise bad research. However, a study cannot be sexist and constitute good research.

There is still a dearth of serious scholarship on many aspects of gender and education, particularly research done by dispassionate, disinterested, ideal researchers of the type described by Morris (1981:163).

> *The ideal researcher.* Somewhere there is someone who is totally objective, has no preconceived notions and who collects data unsullied by selective perception. We seek out this paragon for every project but always find that she is already employed on another project and will not be free for two years.

Among the research areas that need to be studied by such an ideal scholar are many relating to masculinity and education. Research on boys and men in education has now become a paradoxical topic. On the one hand we have educational research on social mobility (Halsey *et al.* 1980), history (Simon 1974a, b), grammar school streaming (Lacey 1970), delinquency and school ethos (Rutter *et al.* 1979), medical student socialization (Becker *et al.* 1961) urban street gangs (Parker 1974) and public school parental choice (Fox 1985). Yet in all these projects the male samples are not studied *as males* who might have different perspectives from females, but as representatives of the UK population, the rise of the working class, the inhumanity of the grammar school, the importance of a good school ethos, the learning environment of medical school, life in an inner-city slum, and the social role of private schooling in modern Britain. When we need to know something about *men's* different experiences compared to *women's*, we typically have no available data. In a society where most people live in a mixed world, and where most educational institutions are mixed, this is distinctly odd. There are many areas of research where data on males *as males* would be of considerable educational value.

Much of the force of feminist critiques of existing educational research has come from pointing out that only half the story is being told. Thus Brian Simon's three-volume history of education in Britain fails to deal with women's education at all (Simon 1965, 1974a, b); the philosophy (Martin 1984); psychology (Sayers 1984) and sociolinguistics (French and French 1984) of education have all been criticized on similar grounds while sociology of education has been particularly censured (Acker 1981). There is no doubt that women and girls have been neglected, and that the accounts offered by the various disciplines are thereby impoverished. Educational administration research has equally neglected women. Casanova (1985), for example, found that *no* research had been done on school secretaries and they were not even mentioned in most administration textbooks. As feminists fill these gaps in our knowledge the lack of work on males as males in education becomes more apparent.

The 1980s saw a series of initiatives in Britain to encourage girls and women into science and technology. Apart from Girls and Technical Education (GATE), Women into Science and Engineering (WISE) and Girls into Science and Technology (GIST), which are well-known attempts to challenge the 'masculine' image of science, there has been a series of Women's Training Roadshows, and a continuing use of WISE buses to visit schools. TVEI and the National Curriculum in England and Wales are also explicitly intended to keep young women involved in scientific and technical subjects at least till 16. The initiatives by engineering organizations to increase awareness of the activity among school pupils, such as Insight courses, Opening Windows and Neighbourhood Engineer, include some programmes directed particularly at young women. Much of this activity has gone without evaluation or monitoring and the impact is therefore unknown. The GIST project was subjected to internal and external research (Whyte 1985), one Roadshow was evaluated (Pilcher *et al.* 1989a, b, c) and TVEI is being scrutinized (Gleeson 1988). However, WISE year, WISE buses,

GATE, Insight, Opening Windows and Neighbourhood Engineer have *not* been evaluated by trained researchers. A proper evaluation programme of all these schemes is needed.

There is also the problem of small samples. Many of the most famous pieces of research (e.g. Stanworth 1983, Okely 1975, Spender 1982), indeed the bulk of the works cited in this book, are small-scale studies of a few pupils done single-handedly by one researcher. As I have argued elsewhere, the sample sizes are too small to support the conclusions drawn from them (see Delamont 1984c). Our knowledge about class inequalities, or teacher-pupil interaction in primary classrooms, or attitudes to chemistry at 14, is based on much larger databases collected by teams of scholars. It is a priority for the 1990s to have data on sex, gender and education gathered on large samples by groups of researchers. This is not a straightforward proposal. The climate is not favourable towards large-scale research on anything educational, there are very few trained researchers dispassionate about sex roles in education, and the studies would have to be conducted carefully to avoid schools trying to present themselves as they thought the research team wanted them to be rather than as they are away from the scholar's gaze. Despite these problems, we must have adequate statistical data.

Finally in this section there is the question of dissemination. Most educational research never reaches educational administrators or teachers, and almost all of it is unknown to parents and pupils. Indeed many researchers do not read enough of the available scholarship. In the 1990s attention has to be paid to disseminating the findings we have already. The best way to reach teachers, pupils and parents would be TV soaps. *Grange Hill* should regularly feature boys facing cries of 'poofter' when they opt for childcare, and girls using physics to meet people. *Neighbours* needs a glamorous woman chemist, and a male nurse who does his own mending. For adults, a series set in the staff common room of a college of higher education or a polytechnic or university with all the bite of *Hill Street Blues* and glamour of *LA Law* would provide powerful drama about sex roles and education, and stories could raise issues and dilemmas stemming from educational research. In such a series women scientists and engineers, and male textile designers and home economics experts, would add to the drama.

This may seem frivolous – but in the 1990s some equally dramatic ways must be found to spread the findings of the research of the 1980s to the wide world.

The future for teachers, schools and pupils

The teacher who wants to rethink the sexism in his or her subject, the pupil who wants to pursue an unusual option and the school which wants to run an in-service day on gender all have a more sympathetic climate and more materials available than they did when the first edition of this book was published. In particular, the *Genderwatch* pack, available in Welsh as well as English, is a marvellous resource for individual teachers and whole schools. There are some books for girls to widen their horizons, and perhaps there will be some for boys too in the near future. However, there are three dangers. First, the enthusiastic minority may be visible, but there is no evidence that the majority of teachers or pupils have seen any problems with the sex-role regime of schools. Secondly, once an in-service day has been 'done', gender may be regarded as 'last year's topic', and so new angles will have to be sought constantly. Thirdly, the shortage of school leavers in the early 1990s may appear to have loosened barriers between women and 'male' jobs, but they are likely to reappear when young men are available again (along with the creches, job sharing and career break schemes currently being lauded). Affirmative action needs to be enshrined in legislation while there is a shortage of male school leavers, so the gains are not lost.

The future for the education system

The impact of the many changes in educational systems and practices introduced during the 1980s is not yet apparent in Northern Ireland, Scotland, Wales or England. Nor is it feasible to predict the changes that may come. Northern Ireland might abandon single-sex schools, and there may be new Islamic girls' schools opened all over the UK. The interrelations between SCOTVEC and gender in Scotland are yet to be seen and will need study. If TVEI actually *achieves* its own aim of challenging gender stereotypes in vocational education the consequences would be considerable. England and Wales are about to see national testing and a National Curriculum (not applicable in Northern Ireland and Scotland or in fee-paying schools or City Technology Colleges (CTCs) in England and Wales, so the term 'National' is odd) and the implications of these for gender inequalities, stereotypes and segregations will need careful monitoring. If the national curriculum means that boys cannot abandon foreign languages and girls drop science and technology until they are able to appreciate their vocational importance, then it may reduce sex differentiation. We have to watch with some scepticism how the national curriculum works out in practice.

Afterword

In 1987, women's cricket celebrated the fiftieth anniversary of test matches against Australia and played at Lords for the second time this century. While men earn large sums of money, and sponsorship provides large prizes, the women paid for themselves, and the trophy was a crystal bowl (Rheinberg 1988). Perhaps in 2001 equal opportunities in schools will have made women's cricket as important and well rewarded as men's.

Further reading

The boom in research and writing on women and education has yet to be matched by much work on men and education in which masculinity is treated as problematic rather than taken for granted. This section is divided into two parts: first books for the general reader who wants to explore the issues, then ideas for anyone wanting to do their own research.

For the general reader

The most interesting books on education and gender are still fictional ones. Three novels remind us about how restricting the ideologies governing women and education were before the Second World War, and are salutary reading: W. Holtby's *South Riding* (1936), Ruth Adam's (1938/1983) *I'm Not Complaining* and Dorothy L. Sayers (1935) *Gaudy Night*. Both the first two focus on teachers trying to enlighten the working class and face up to spinsterhood, the Sayers is about sexuality and scholarship in higher education.

Amanda Cross has written a series of books featuring a female don (Kate Fansler) all of which raise issues about gender and learning. *The Theban Mysteries* is about a girls' school; *A Death in the Faculty* and *Sweet Death, Kind Death* deal with women in universities and the rise of women's studies, while *The Question of Max* and *No Word from Winifred* are reworkings of those issues among earlier generations of women.

Among research studies the best book on gender and education is Raphaela Best's (1983) *We've all got Scars*. Illuminating about boys are Gary Alan Fine's (1987) *With the Boys*, and Carl Grant and Christine Sleeter's (1986) *After the School Bell*

Rings. From Australia Bob Connell and his colleagues have produced *Teachers' Work* and *Making The Difference* which deal with sex roles both among staff and pupils and reveal class differences in sex-role patterns.

Research sources

Bibliographies

Kay Wilkins' (1979) *Women's Education in the United States* is a bibliography of 1134 items on women's education in the USA.

Gaby Weiner and Madeline Arnot (1988) *Gender and Education* is an excellent UK bibliography, available from The Open University, London Region, Parsifal College, 527 Kinchley Road, London NW3 7BG for £5.00.

David Ford and Jeff Hearn (1988) *Studying Men and Masculinity*, University of Bradford, Applied Social Studies. This has sections on childhood and schooling, though they have fewer items noted than this book!

Women in Scotland: an Annotated Bibliography. This is prepared by a group who welcome suggestions for additions. Available from: The Women in Scotland Bibliography Group, c/o The Open University in Scotland, 60 Melville Street, Edinburgh EH3 7HF.

There is no equivalent source on Wales, but *Contemporary Wales* vol. 2 (1988) has a paper by Peter Ellis Jones on Welsh secondary education with a short section on gender.

Steven Walker and Len Barton (eds) (1983) *Gender, Class and Education* has three excellent bibliographies at the end, on the USA, on Australia and New Zealand, and on Europe.

Books on research

In Britain, Rosemary Deem and Gaby Weiner edit a series called Gender and Education published by the Open University Press. These are good on English (but not Welsh, Scottish or Irish) issues and cheap. So far eight titles are available: Askew and Ross (1988) *Boys Don't Cry*, Brown and France (1983) *Untying* the Apron Strings, Burchell and Millman (1989) *Changing Perspectives on Gender,* Deem (1984) *Coeducation Reconsidered,* De Lyon and Migniuolo (1989) *Women Teachers,* Holly (1989) *Girls and Sexuality,* Weiner (1985) *Just a Bunch of Girls* and Wickham (1985) *Women and Training.*

Longmans publish a series of large booklets reporting Schools Council work and thinking on gender. These include:

Muriel Eddowes (1983) *Humble Pi: The Mathematics Education of Girls*

Jan Harding (1983) *Switched Off: The Science Education of Girls*

John Catton (1984) *Ways and Means: The CDT Education of Girls*

Rosemary Stones (1983) *Pour Out the Cocoa, Janet* (children's books)

Judith Whyte (1983) *Beyond the Wendy House* (primary schools)

Oliver Leaman (1984) *Sit on the Sidelines and Watch the Boys Play* (PE)

Rich and Phillips (eds) (1985) *Women's Experience and Education* is a compilation of the best from *Harvard Educational Review.*

Two volumes from the Open University Press lead into the research going on: Arnot and Weiner (eds) (1987) *Gender and the Politics of Schooling,* Weiner and Arnot (eds) (1987) *Gender under Scrutiny*

Klein (ed.) (1985) *Handbook for Achieving Sex Equity through Education*

Acker *et al.* (eds) (1984) *Women and Education* (as this is a world yearbook, it covers a wide range of societies)

On research methods

Eichler (1988) *Nonsexist Research Methods*

Harding (1987) *Feminism and Methodology*

Stanley and Wise (1983) *Breaking Out*

Richardson and Wirtenberg (eds) (1983) *Sex Role Research.*

Monitoring/changing your own institution

Genderwatch, devised by Kate Myers for the SCDC, is splendid. It is full of ideas for examining your own workplace and thoughts on changing it. (It is available in Welsh from Clwyd CC, and in English from SCDC, Newcombe House, 45 Notting Hill Gate, London W11 3JB for about £3.50.)

The NUT have published a resource pack *Towards Equality for Girls and Boys* available from Hamilton House, London.

For primary schools particularly Dorothy Walker (1986) *Gender Equality* has lots of exercises and splendid illustrations of milkwomen and men making beds.

TVEI Developments 2 – *Equal Opportunities*. Free to teachers from TVEI Information Point, 236 Gray's Inn Road, London WC1X 8HL

Whyld, J. (ed.) (1983) *Sexism in the Secondary Curriculum*.

Journals and periodicals

There are several journals devoted to scholarship on gender: *Gender and Education* (volume 1, 1989) is a new British journal; *Signs* is the classic American journal of feminist scholarship which includes some educational material; see also *Women's Studies International Forum*, *Sex Roles*, and *Gender and Society* (volume 1, 1987) the official journal of the American group Sociologists for Women in Society.

Many educational journals have had special issues on gender in the past decade. For example: *Contemporary Issues in Geography and Education* vol. 3 no. 1 (1989) is a special issue on gender and geography, *British Journal of Religious Education* vol. 12 no. 1 (1989) is on women's studies, and the *Internationl Review of Education* vol. 33 no. 4 (1987) is on women. *Sociology of Education* vol. 62 no. 1 January 1989 was a special issue on gender, and the *British Journal of Sociology of Education* regularly contains articles on gender issues.

It is worth scanning the journals in your particular area, such as geography, or music or maths, to see if there has been such an issue in the past 5 or 6 years. If there hasn't, write to the editor and suggest one!

Bibliography and name index

Arnot, M. and Weiner, G. (eds) (1987) *Gender and the Politics of Schooling*, Milton Keynes: Open University Press. *120*

Arscott, C. *et al.* (eds) (1937) *The Headmistress Speaks*, London: Kegan Paul, Trench, Trubner. *127*

Ashton, P. (1981) 'Primary teachers' aims 1969–1977', in B. Simon and J. Willcocks (eds) *Research and Practice in the Primary Classroom*, London: Routledge & Kegan Paul. *30*

Ashton, P. *et al.* (1975) *The Aims of Primary Education*, London: Macmillan. *30*

Askew, S. and Ross, C. (1988) *Boys Don't Cry: Boys and Sexism in Education*, Milton Keynes: Open University Press. *101, 119–20*

Atkinson, P.A. and Delamont, S. (1985a) 'Socialization into teaching: the research which lost its way', *British Journal of Sociology of Education* 6 (3): 307–22. *68, 73*

Atkinson, P.A. and Delamont, S. (1985b) 'Bread and dreams or bread and circuses: a critique of "case study" research in education', in M. Shipman (ed.) *Educational Research: Principles, Policies and Practices*, London: Falmer. *16*

Atkinson, P.A. and Delamont, S. (1990) 'Professions and powerlessness', *Sociological Review* 38 (1). *90–110*

Atkinson, P.A., Delamont, S. and Beynon, J. (1988a) 'In the beginning was the bunsen', *Qualitative Studies in Education* 1 (4): 315–28. *98*

Atkinson, P.A., Delamont, S. and Hammersley, M. (1988b) 'Qualitative research traditions: a British response to Jacob', *Review of Educational Research* 58 (2): 67 231–50. *67*

Ball, S. (1981) *Beachside Comprehensive*, Cambridge: The University Press. *49*

Ball, S. (1987) *The Micro-Politics of the School*, London: Methuen. *67, 79*

Ball, S. and Goodson, I. (eds) (1984) *Teachers' Lives and Careers*, London: Falmer. *67–8*

Banks, O. (1968) *The Sociology of Education*, London: Batsford.

Barker, D.L. and Allen, S. (eds) (1976a) *Dependence and Exploitation in Work and Marriage*, London: Longman. *142, 145*

Barnes, D. and Todd, F. (1977) *Communication and Learning in*

Small Groups, London: Routledge & Kegan Paul. *58*

Baruch, G.K. (1974) 'Sex-role attitudes of fifth grade girls', in Stacey *et al.* (eds) *And Jill Came Tumbling After*, New York: Dell. *64*

Becker, H.S. *et al.* (1961) *Boys in White*, Chicago: The University Press. *113*

Bell, C. and Howieson, C. (1988) 'The view from the hutch', in D. Raffe (ed.) *Education and the Youth Labour Market*, London: Falmer. *100*

Best, R. (1983) *We've All Got Scars*, Bloomington, IN: Indiana University Press. *5, 23, 28, 33, 37, 38, 41, 51, 58, 105, 118*

Beynon, J. (1985a) *Initial Encounters in the Secondary School*, London: Falmer. *47, 76*

Beynon, J. (1985b) 'Career histories in a comprehensive school', in S. Ball and I. Goodson (eds) *Teachers' Lives and Careers*, London: Falmer. *1*

Beynon, J. (1987) 'Miss Floral mends her ways', in L. Tickle (ed.) *The Arts in Education*, London: Croom Helm. *66*

Beynon, J. (1989) 'A school for men', in S. Walker and L. Barton (eds) *Politics and the Processes of Schooling*, Milton Keynes: Open University Press.

Blackburn, R.M. and Mann, M. (1979) *The Working Class in the Labour Market*, London: Macmillan. *70, 106*

Bossert, S. (1983) 'Understanding sex differences in children's classroom experience', in W. Doyle and T. Good (eds) *Focus on Teaching*, Chicago: The University Press. *26*

Bowles, G. and Duelli Klein, R. (eds) (1983) *Theories of Women's Studies*, London: Routledge & Kegan Paul. *111*

Braman, Olive (1977) 'Comics' in J. King and M. Stott (1977) (eds) *Is This Your Life?*, London: Virago.

Brelsford, P., Rix, A. and Smith, G. (1982) 'Give us a break: widening opportunities for young women within YOP/YTS', *Research and Development Series No. 11*, Manpower Services Commission. *4*

Bright, D. (1987) *Teachers' Morale*, Unpublished MEd thesis, University College, Cardiff. *69*

Brod, H. (ed.) (1987) *The Making of Masculinities*. London: Allen & Unwin. *126*

Brophy, J. (1985) 'Interactions of male and female students with male and female teachers', in L.C. Wilkinson and C.B. Marrett, (eds) *Gender Influences in Classroom Interaction*, Orlando, FL: Academic Press. *26*

Brophy, J.E. and Good, T.L. (1974) *Teacher-Student Relationships*, New York: Holt Rinehart & Winston. *26*

Browne, J. (1979) *Teachers of Teachers*, London: Hodder & Stoughton. *89*

Brown, J. *et al.* (eds) (1986) *Science in Schools*, Milton Keynes: Open University Press. *142*

Brown, N. and France, P. (eds) (1983) *Untying the Apron Strings*, Milton Keynes: Open University Press. *120*

Brunvand, H.J. (1983) *The Vanishing Hitchhiker*, London: Picador. *41*

Bryan, K.A (1980) 'Pupil perceptions of transfer' in A. Hargreaves and L. Tickle (eds) *Middle Schools*, London: Harper & Row. *43*

Bullivant, B.M. (1978) *The Way of Tradition*, Victoria: ACER.

Burchell, H. and Millman, V. (eds) (1989) *Changing Perspectives on Gender*, Milton Keynes: Open University Press. *99, 101, 120*

Burgess, R.G. (1983) *Experiencing Comprehensive Education*, London: Tavistock. *4*

Burgess, R.G. (1988) 'Whatever happened to the Newsom course?', in A. Pollard, J. Purvis and G. Walford (eds) *Education, Training and the New Vocationalism*, Milton Keynes: Open University Press. *4*

Burgess, R.G. (1989) 'The politics of pastoral care', in S. Walker and L. Barton (eds) *The Politics and Processes of Schooling*, Milton Keynes: Open University Press. *4*

Burrage, H. (1983) 'Women university teachers of natural science 1971–72', *Social Studies of Science* 13: 147–60. *101*

Buswell, C. (1981) 'Sexism in school routines and classroom practice', *Durham and Newcastle Research Review* 9 46: 195–200. *56–7, 60*

Buswell, C. (1988) 'Flexible workers for flexible firms?', in A. Pollard, J. Purvis and G. Walford (eds) *Education, Training and the New Vocationalism*, Milton Keynes: Open University Press. *106*

Butler, O. (ed.) (1984) *Feminist Experience and Feminist*

Research, Manchester: The Sociology Department, University of Manchester. *111*

Byrne, E. (1978) *Women and Education*, London: Tavistock. *90, 100*

Canaan, J. (1986) 'Why a "slut" is a "slut"', in H. Varenne (ed.) *Symbolizing America*, Lincoln, NB: University of Nebraska Press. *65*

Canaan, J. (1987) 'A comparative analysis of American suburban middle class, middle school and high school teenage cliques', in G. Spindler and L. Spindler (eds) *Interpretive Ethnography of Education*, Hillside, NJ: Lawrence Erlbaum. *65*

Carrigan, T., Connell, B. and Lee, J. (1987) 'Toward a new sociology of masculinity', in H. Brod (ed.) *The Making of Masculinities*, London: Allen & Unwin. *67*

Casanova, U. (1985) Unpublished PhD thesis, University of Arizona. *114*

Catton, J. (1984) *Ways and Means*, London: Longman. *120*

Charlesworth, K. and Cameron, M. (1986) *All That: The Other Half of History*, London: Pandora. *91*

Clarke, M.G. (1937) 'Feminine challenge in education', in C. Arscott, *et al.* (eds) *The Headmistress Speaks*, London: Kegan Paul, Trench, Trubner. *81*

Clarricoates, K. (1980) 'The importance of being Ernest, Emma, Tom, Jane', in R. Deem (ed.) *Schooling for Women's Work*, London: Routledge & Kegan Paul. *23*

Clarricoates, K. (1981) 'The experience of patriarchal schooling', *Interchange* 12 (2/3): 185–206. *23*

Clarricoates, K. (1987) 'Child culture at school: a clash between gendered worlds?', in A. Pollard (ed.) *Children and their Primary Schools*, London: Falmer. *37, 38, 40*

Clarricoates, K. (1989) *Gender and Power in the Primary School*, Cambridge: Polity. *23*

Clegg, S. (1985) ' Feminist methodology', *Quality and Quantity* 19 (1): 83–97. *111*

Cockburn, C. (1987) *Two Track Training*, London: Macmillan. *4, 103, 107*

Coffield, F. *et al.* (1986) *Growing up at the Margins*, Milton Keynes: Open University Press. *45, 52, 53, 106*

Cohen, L. and Manion, L. (1989) *Research Methods in Educa-*

tion, 3rd edn, London: Routledge.

Collard, J. and Mansfield, P. (1987) *The Beginning of the Rest of Your Life?*, London: Macmillan. *5*

Connell, R.W. (1985) *Teachers' Work*, Sydney: Allen & Unwin. *5, 67, 74, 75, 79, 119*

Connell, R.W. (1987) *Gender and Power*, Cambridge: Polity. *51*

Connell, R.W. *et al.* (1982) *Making the Difference*, Sydney: Allen & Unwin. *53, 66, 119*

Corr, H. (1987) 'Sexual politics in the NUT 1870–1920', in P. Summerfield (ed.) *Women, Education and the Professions*, Leicester: History of Education Society. *80*

Cowell, A., Rees, T.L. and Read, M. (1981) 'Occupational aspirations and rising unemployment in a South Wales valley', *Education for Development* 6: 14–24. *96*

Crapanzano, V. (1985) *Waiting*, London: Granada. *9*

Crehan, K. (1986) 'Women, work and the balancing act', in T.S. Epstein, K. Crehan, A. Gerzer and J. Sass (eds) *Women, Work and Family in Britain and Germany*, London: Croom Helm. *70*

Cross, A. (1972) *The Theban Mysteries*, London: Gollancz. *118*

Cross, A. (1976) *The Question of Max*, London: Gollancz. *118*

Cross, A. (1981) *A Death in the Faculty*, London: Gollancz. *118*

Cross, A. (1984) *Sweet Death, Kind Death*, New York: Random House. *118*

Cross, A. (1986) *No Word from Winifred*, London: Virago. *118*

Cunnison, S. (1989) 'Gender joking in the staffroom', in S. Acker (ed.) *Teachers, Gender and Careers*, London: Falmer. *75, 79, 81*

Dale, A. (1987) 'Occupational inequality, gender and the life cycle', *Work Employment and Society* 1 (3): 326–51. *87*

Dale, R.R. (1969) *Mixed or Single Sex School?* vol.1, London: Routledge & Kegan Paul. *87*

Dale, R.R. (1971) *Mixed or Single Sex School?* vol.2, London: Routledge & Kegan Paul. *87*

Dale, R R. (1974) *Mixed or Single Sex School?* vol.3, London:* Routledge & Kegan Paul. *87*

Davidson, H. (1985) 'Unfriendly myths about women teachers', in J. Whyte *et al.* (eds) *Girl Friendly Schooling*, London: Methuen. *82, 83–4, 84–5, 86*

Davie, R. *et al.* (1972) *From Birth to Seven*, London: Longman. *25*

Davies, L. (1984) *Pupil Power*, London: Falmer. *46*

Davies, M. (1937) 'The county secondary school and its service to the community', in C. Arscott *et al.* (eds) *The Headmistress Speaks*, London: Kegan Paul, Trench, Trubner. *81*

Deem, R. (1978) *Women and Schooling*, London: Routledge & Kegan Paul.

Deem, R. (ed.) (1980) *Schooling for Women's Work*, London: Routledge & Kegan Paul.

Deem, R. (ed.) (1984) *Coeducation Reconsidered*, Milton Keynes: Open University Press. *120*

Deem, R. (1986) *All Work and No Play?*, Milton Keynes: Open University Press. *87*

Delamont, S. (1976a) *Interaction in the Classroom*, London: Methuen.

Delamont, S. (1976b) 'The girls most likely to: cultural reproduction and Scottish elites', *Scottish Journal of Sociology* 1 (1): 29–43. *48*

Delamont, S. (1980a) *The Sociology of Women: An Introduction*, London: Allen & Unwin.

Delamont, S. (1980b) *Sex Roles and the School*, London: Methuen. *4, 56*

Delamont, S. (1981) 'All too familiar?', *Educational Analysis* 3 (1): 69–84. *4*

Delamont, S. (1982) 'Sex differences in classroom interaction', *EOC Research Bulletin* 6: 30–7. *4*

Delamont, S. (1983a) 'The conservative school', in L. Barton and S. Walker (eds) *Gender, Class and Education*, London: Falmer. *4*

Delamont, S. (1983b) 'A woman's place in education: myths, monsters and misapprehensions' (Presidential address to BERA), *Research Intelligence* 14: 2–4. *4*

Delamont, S. (1983c) *Interaction in the Classroom*, 2nd edn, London: Methuen. *6, 22*

Delamont, S. (1984a) 'The old girl network', in R.G. Burgess (ed.) *The Research Process in Educational Settings*, London: Falmer. *4, 48, 49*

Delamont, S. (1984b) 'Lessons from St. Luke's', in W.B.

Dockrell (ed.) *An Attitude of Mind*, Edinburgh: SCRE. *4, 48*

Delamont, S. (1984c) 'Sex roles and schooling: or, "See Janet suffer, see John suffer too" ', *Journal of Adolescence* 7: 329–35. *5, 63, 76, 115*

Delamont, S. (1984d) *Readings on Interaction in the Classroom*, London: Methuen.

Delamont, S. (1986) 'Discussion: a view from a quadruple outsider', *Teaching and Teacher Education* 2 (4): 329–32.

Delamont, S. (1987a) 'The primary teacher 1945–1990', in S. Delamont (ed.) *The Primary School Teacher*, London: Falmer. *67, 86–7*

Delamont, S. (1987b) 'Three blind spots?', *Social Studies of Science* 17 (1): 163–170. *101*

Delamont, S. (1989a) 'Both sexes lose out', in A. Ramasut (ed.) *Whole School Approaches to Special Needs*, London: Falmer. *100*

Delamont, S. (1989b) 'The nun in the toilet', *Qualitative Studies in Education* 2 (3) 191–202. *10, 43*

Delamont, S. (1989c) 'The fingernail on the blackboard', *Studies in Science Education* 16: 25–46. *101*

Delamont, S. (1989d) *Knowledgeable Women*, London: Routledge. *46, 49*

Delamont, S. (1991) *Fieldwork in Educational Settings*, London: Falmer, in press. *111*

Delamont, S. and Duffin, L. (eds) (1978) *The Nineteenth Century Woman*, London: Croom Helm.

Delamont, S. and Galton, M. (1986) *Inside the Secondary Classroom*, London: Routledge & Kegan Paul. *10, 15, 27, 41–2, 43, 51, 56, 58*

Delamont, S. and Galton, M. (1987) 'Anxieties and anticipations', in A. Pollard (ed.) *Children and Their Primary Schools*, London: Croom Helm.' *43*

Delamont, S. and Hamilton, D. (1984) 'Revisiting classroom research', in S. Delamont (ed.) *Readings on Interaction in the Classroom*, London: Methuen.

De Lyon, M. and Migniuolo, F.W. (eds) (1989) *Women Teachers*, Milton Keynes: Open University Press. *68, 120*

Dennis, N. *et al.* (1957) *Coal is Our Life*, London: Eyre & Spottiswoode. *70*

Denscombe, M. (1985) *Classroom Control*, London: Allen & Unwin. *67*

Doherty, M. (1987) 'Science education for girls', *School Science Review* 69 246: 28–33. *101*

Douglas, J.W.B. (1964) *The Home and the School*, London: MacGibbon & Kee. *25*

Dove, L. (1975) 'The hopes of immigrant school children', *New Society* 10 April: 63–5. *53*

Driver, G. (1979) 'Classroom stress and school achievement', in V.S. Khan (ed.) *Minority Families in Britain*, London: Macmillan.

Driver, R. (1983) *The Pupil as Scientist*, Milton Keynes: Open University Press. *109*

Eddowes, M. (1983) *Humble Pi*, London: Longman. *120*

Eggleston, S.J. (1974) 'Sex and the single schools', *Times Educational Supplement* 10 June 1974.

Eichler, M. (1988) *Nonsexist Research Methods*, Boston: Allen & Unwin. *111, 113, 120*

Elliot, J. (1974) 'Sex roles and silence in the classroom', *Spare Rib* 27: 12–15. *58*

Elliot, K. (1978) 'Diary of a feminist teacher', *Spare Rib* 75: 20–1. *75*

Epstein, C. (1983) *Women in Law*, New York: Doubleday. *87*

Equal Opportunities Commission (1987) *Women and Men in Britain 1986*, London: HMSO.

Equal Opportunities Commission (1989) *Formal Investigation Report: Initial Teacher Training in England and Wales*, Manchester: EOC. *73*

Farrell, C. (1978) *My Mother Said*, London: Routledge & Kegan Paul. *52*

Fawcett Society (1987) *Exams for the Boys*, London: privately printed. *62*

Fevre, R. (1988) Personal communication. *21*

Fine, G.A. (1981) 'Rude words', *Maledicta* 5: 51–68. *41*

Fine, G.A. (1987) *With The Boys*, Chicago: The University Press. *41, 118*

Flanders, N. A. (1970) *Analysing Teaching Behaviour*, Reading, MΛ: Addison-Wesley.

Flecker, J.E. (1922) *Hassan*, London: Heinemann. *111–12*

Flecker, J.E. (1946) *Collected Poems*, London: Martin Secker. *41*

Fletcher, S. (1984) *Women First*, London: Athlone. *88*

Fogelman, K. (1976) *Britain's Sixteen Year Olds*, London: National Children's Bureau.

Ford, D. and Hearn, J. (1988) *Studying Men and Masculinity*, Bradford: University of Bradford. *119*

Fox, I. (1985) *Private Schools and Public Issues*, London: Macmillan. *113*

French, J. and French, P. (1984) 'Sociolinguistics and gender divisions', in S. Acker *et al.* (eds) *Women and Education*, London: Kogan Page. *114*

Frosch, M. (1976) 'Observing a pre-school class', in M. Guttentag and H. Bray (eds) *Undoing Sex Stereotypes. Research and Resources for Educators*, New York: McGraw-Hill.

Fuller, M. (1980) 'Black girls in a London comprehensive', in R. Deem (ed.) *Schooling for Women's Work*, London: Routledge & Kegan Paul. *48*

Furlong, V.J. (1976) 'Interaction sets in the classroom', in M. Stubbs and S. Delamont (eds) *Explorations in Classroom Observation*, Chichester: Wiley. *48*

Furlong, V.J. (1984) 'Black resistance in the liberal comprehensive', in S. Delamont (ed.) *Readings on Interaction in the Classroom*, London: Methuen. *48*

Galloway, H. M. (1973) Female students and their aspirations, Unpublished MPhil. thesis, University of Edinburgh. *70-2, 73*

Galton, M. and Willcocks, J. (eds) (1983) *Moving from the Primary Classroom*, London: Routledge & Kegan Paul. *56*

Gibson, M. (1987a) 'The school performance of immigrant minorities', *Anthropology and Education Quarterly* 18 (4): 62–75. *105-6*

Gibson, M. (1987b) 'Punjabi immigrants in an American high school', in G. and L. Spindler (eds) *Interpretive Ethnography of Education*, Hillsdale, NJ: Erlbaum. *105-6*

Gilbert, J. and Watts, M. (1983) 'Concepts, misconceptions and alternative conceptions', *Studies in Science Education* 10: 61–98. *109*

Gillborn, D. (1987) Unpublished PhD thesis, University of

Nottingham. *58*

Gilligan, C. (1982) *In a Different Voice*, Cambridge, MA: Harvard University Press. *6*

Ginsburg, M. *et al.* (1977) *The Role of the Middle School Teacher*, Aston Educational Enquiry Monographs, 7. Birmingham: University of Aston. *78-9*

Gleeson, D. (ed.) (1987) *T.V.E.I. and Secondary Education*, Milton Keynes: Open University Press. *114*

Gold, B.A. and Miles, M. B. (1981) *Whose School is it Anyway?* New York: Praeger. *2*

Goldthorpe, J. *et al.* (1969) *The Affluent Worker in the Class Structure*, Cambridge: The University Press.

Good, T.L. (1987) 'Teacher expectations', in D. Berliner and B. Rosenshine (eds) *Talks to Teachers*, New York: Teachers College Press. *26, 73*

Goodman, L.W. *et al.* (1974) 'A report on children's toys', in J. Stacey *et al.* (eds) *And Jill Came Tumbling After*, New York: Dell. *19*

Grace, G. (1972) *Teachers, Ideology and Control*, London: Routledge & Kegan Paul. *74*

Grant, C. and Sleeter, C. (1986) *After the School Bell Rings*, London: Falmer. *118-19*

Grauerholz, E. and Pescosolido, B.A. (1989) 'Gender representation in children's literature', *Gender and Society* 3 (1): 113–25. *21*

Griffin, C. (1985) *Typical Girls?*, London: Routledge & Kegan Paul. *46*

Griffiths, V. (1986) *Using Drama To Get At Gender*, Studies in Sexual Politics series, 9, Manchester: University of Manchester.

Guttentag, M. and Bray, H. (eds) (1976) *Undoing Sex Stereotypes. Research and Resources for Educators*, New York: McGraw-Hill. *5, 37, 94*

Hall, S. and Jefferson, T. (eds) (1975) *Resistance through Rituals*, London: Hutchinson. *45*

Halsey, A.H., Heath, A. and Ridge, J.M. (1980) *Origins and Destinations*, Oxford: Clarendon Press. *113*

Hamilton, D. (1977) *In Search of Structure*, London: Hodder & Stoughton. *23*

Hammersley, M. and Atkinson, P.A. (1983) *Ethnography: Principles in Practice*, London: Tavistock. *112*

Hanson, D. and Herrington, M. (1976a) 'Please Miss, you're supposed to stop her', *New Society* 10 June: 568–9. *75*

Hanson, D. and Herrington, M. (1976b) *From College to Classroom*, London: Routledge & Kegan Paul. *75*

Harding, J. (1983) *Switched Off*, London: Longman. *120*

Harding, J. (ed.) (1986) *Perspectives on Gender and Science*, London: Falmer. *101*

Harding, S. (ed.) (1986) *The Science Question in Feminism*, Milton Keynes: Open University Press. *101*

Harding, S. (ed.) (1987) *Feminism and Methodology*, London: Falmer. *120*

Harding, S. and O'Barr, J.F. (eds) (1987) *Sex and Scientific Inquiry*, Chicago: The University Press. *101*

Hargreaves, D. (1967) *Social Relations in a Secondary School*, London: Routledge & Kegan Paul. *47, 48, 53*

Hargreaves, D., Hester, S.K. and Mellor, F.J. (1975) *Deviance in Classrooms*, London: Routledge & Kegan Paul. *49, 76, 77*

Harrison, B.G. (1973) *Unlearning the Lie*, *111*New York: Liveright.

Harrison, L. (1975) 'Cro-Magnon woman – in eclipse', *Science Teacher* 42 (4): 9–11. *62*

Hart, R.A. (1979) *Children's Experience of Place: A Developmental Study*, New York: Irvington. *20*

Hartley, D. (1978) 'Sex and social class: A case study of an infant school', *British Educational Research Journal* 4 (2): 75–82. *25–6*

Heath, A. (1981) *Social Mobility*, London: Fontana. *89–90*

Hendry, E. (1987) *Exams for the Boys*, London: The Fawcett Society. *62*

Hill, S. (1976) *The Dockers*, London: Heinemann. *70*

Hilsum, S. and Start, K.B. (1974) *Promotion and Careers in Teaching*, Slough: NFER. *69, 83, 85, 87–8*

HMI (1979) *Aspects of Secondary Education*, London: HMSO. *81*

Holland, J. (1988) 'Girls and occupational choice', in A. Pollard, J. Purvis and G. Walford (eds) *Education, Training and the New*

Vocationalism, Milton Keynes: Open University Press. *54–5*

Holly, L. (ed.) (1989) *Girls and Sexuality*, Milton Keynes: Open University Press. *120*

Holtby, W. (1936) *South Riding*, reprinted 1974, Glasgow: Fontana. *118*

Horner, M. S. (1971) 'Femininity and successful achievement: a basic inconsistency', in M. Garskof (ed.) *Roles Women Play*, California: Brooks/Cole.

Howson, G. (1982) *History of Mathematical Education in England*, Cambridge: The University Press. *88*

ILEA (1984) *Providing Equal Opportunity for Girls and Boys in Physical Education*, London: ILEA.

Ingelby, J.D. and Cooper, E. (1974) 'How teachers perceive first-year schoolchildren', *Sociology* 8 (3): 463–73. *25*

Jayaratne, T.E. (1983) 'The value of quantitative methodology for feminist research', in G. Bowles and R. Duelli Klein (eds) *Theories of Women's Studies*, London: Routledge & Kegan Paul. *112*

Joffe, C. (1971) 'Sex role socialization and the nursery school', *Journal of Marriage and the Family* 33 (3). *27, 38*

Joffe, C. (1974) 'As the twig is bent', in J. Stacey, *et al.* (eds) *And Jill Came Tumbling After*, New York: Dell. *36*

Jones, C.L. and McPherson, A. (1972) 'Do they choose or are they pushed?', *Times Educational Supplement* (Scotland) 9 June: 76. *72–3*

Jones, E. (1988) 'Improving the formula', *Times Educational Supplement* 23 September: 25. *102*

Jones, I. (1974) Unpublished dissertation, University of Leicester. *46*

Jones, P.E. (1989) 'Some trends in Welsh secondary education 1967–1987', *Contemporary Wales* 2: 99–117. *119*

Joyce, M. (1987) 'Being a feminist teacher', in M. Lawn and G. Grace (eds) *Teachers: The Culture and Politics of Work*, London: Falmer. *75*

Karkau, K. (1976) 'A student teacher in 4th grade', in M. Guttentag and H. Bray (1976) (eds) *Undoing Sex Stereotypes. Research and Resources for Educator*, New York: McGraw-Hill. *38*

Keddie, N. (1971) 'Classroom knowledge', in M.F.D. Young

(ed.) *Knowledge and Control*, London: Collier-Macmillan. *102*

Keillor, G. (1986) *Lake Wobegon Days*, London: Faber & Faber. *103*

Keller, E.F. (1985) *Reflections on Gender and Science*, New Haven, CT: Yale University Press. *101*

Kelly, A. (1981) (ed.) *The Missing Half*, Manchester: The University Press. *101*

Kelly, A. (1985a) 'The construction of masculine science', *British Journal of the Sociology of Education* 6 (2): 133-54. *101*

Kelly, A. (1985b) 'Traditionalists and trendies', *British Educational Research Journal* 11 (2): 91-104. *75*

Kelly, A. (1988) 'Ethnic differences in science choice, attitudes and achievement in Britain', *British Education Research Journal* 14 (2): 113-27.

Kelsall, K. *et al.* (1972) *Graduates*, London: Methuen. *52*

King, S. (1987). 'Feminists in teaching', in M. Lawn and G. Grace (eds) *Teachers*, London: Falmer. *80*

King, J. and Stott, M. (eds) (1977) *Is This Your Life?*, London: Virago.

King, R. (1971) 'Unequal access in education', *Social and Economic Administration* 5 (3): 167-74.

King, R. (1978) *All Things Bright and Beautiful*, Chichester: Wiley. *23, 27, 28, 29, 32-3*

Klein, S.S. (ed.) (1985) *Handbook for Achieving Sex Equity through Education* Baltmore: Johns Hopkins University Press. *120*.

Komorovsky, M. (1946) 'Cultural contradictions and sex roles', *American Journal of Sociology* 52: 182-9. *71*

Komorovsky, M. (1972) 'Cultural contradictions and sex roles: the masculine case', in J. Huber (ed.) *Changing Women in a Changing Society*, Chicago: The University Press. *71*

Kuvlesky, W.P. and Bealer, R.C. (1972) 'A clarification of the concept "occupational choice" ', in R.M. Pavalko (ed.) *Sociological Perspectives on Occupations*, Itasca. IL: Peacock. *96*

Lacey, C. (1970) *Hightown Grammar; The School as Social System*, Manchester: The University Press. *47, 113*

Lacey, C. (1977) *The Socialization of Teachers*, London: Methuen. *68, 74*

Lambart, A. (1977) 'The sisterhood', in M. Hammersley and P. Woods (eds) *Process of Schooling*, London: Routledge & Kegan Paul. *48*

Lambart, A. (1980) 'Expulsion in context', in R. Frankenberg (ed.) *Custom and Conflict in British Society*, Manchester: The University Press. *48*

Lawn, M. and Grace, G. (eds) (1987) *Teachers: The Culture and Politics of Work*, London: Falmer. *68*

Laytor, D. (1984) *Interpreters of Science*, London: Murray.

Leaman, O. (1984) *Sit on the Sidelines and Watch the Boys Play: Sex Differences in Physical Education*, London: Longman. *120*

Lees, S. (1986) *Losing Out*, London: Heinemann. *45, 49, 50*

Lightfoot, S. L. (1975) 'Sociology of education: perspectives on women', in M. Millman and R.M. Kanter (eds) *Another Voice*, New York: Anchor Books. *79*

Lindow, J., Marrett, C.B. and Wilkinson, L.C. (1985) 'Overview', in L.C. Wilkinson and C.B. Marrett (eds) *Gender Influences in Classroom Interaction*, Orlando, FL: Academic Press. *23*

Llewellyn, M. (1980) 'Studying girls at school', in R. Deem (ed.) *Schooling for Women's Work*, London: Routlege & Kegan Paul. *48*

Lobban, G. (1974) 'Presentation of sex roles in British reading schemes', *Forum* 16 (2): 57–60. *20*

Lobban, G. (1975) 'Sex roles in reading schemes', *Educational Review* 27 (3): 202–10. *20*

Lofland, J. (1971) *Analysing Social Settings*, Belmont, CA: Wadsworth. *112*

Lorber, J. (1984) *Women and Medicine*, London: Tavistock. *87*

Lubeck, S. (1985) *Sandbox Society*, London: Falmer. *28, 33*

Maccia, E. S. *et al.* (eds) (1975) *Women and Education*, New York: Thomas. *20*

McLaren, P. (1986) *Schooling as Ritual Performance*, New York: Routledge & Kegan Paul.

McGann, O. (1987) Unpublished fieldnotes/Personal communication. *93–4*

Maciuszko, W. (1978) 'Just a stage' *Spare Rib* 75: 17. *75*

McNeill, M. (ed.) (1988) *Gender and Expertise*, London: Verso. *101*

McRobbie, A. (1978) 'Working class girls and the culture of femininity', in *Contemporary Cultural Studies II: Women Take Issue*, London: Hutchinson. *45*

McRobbie, A. (1990) *Feminism and Youth Culture*, London: Macmillan. *45*

McRobbie, A. and Garber, J. (1975) 'Girls and subcultures', in *Cultural Studies*, 7/8 (Summer) and in S. Hall and T. Jefferson (eds) *Resistance through Rituals*, London: Hutchinson. *45*

McRobbie, A. and McCabe, T. (eds) (1981) *Feminism for Girls*, London: Routledge & Kegan Paul. *45*

Manthorpe, C.A. (1982) 'Men's science, women's science or science?', *Studies in Science Education* 9: 65–80. *101*

Marsland, D. (1983) 'Youth', in A. Hartnett (ed.) *The Social Sciences in Educational Studies*, London: Heinemann. *46*

Martin, J.R. (1984) *Reclaiming a Conversation*, New Haven, CT: Yale University Press. *6, 114*

Measor, L. (1984) 'Gender and the sciences' in M. Hammersley and P. Woods (eds) *Life in School*, Milton Keynes: Open University Press. *65*

Measor, L. (1989) 'Are you coming to see some dirty films today?', in L. Holly (ed.) *Girls and Sexuality*, Milton Keynes, Open University Press. *50, 65, 110*

Measor, L. and Woods, P. (1983) 'The interpretation of pupil myths', in M. Hammersley (ed.) *The Ethnography of Schooling*, Driffield, Yorks: Wafferton Books. *43*

Measor, L. and Woods, P. (1984) *Changing Schools*, Milton Keynes: Open University Press. *42-3, 51*

Meyenn, R. J. (1980) 'School girls' peer groups', in P. Woods (ed.) *Pupil Strategies*, London: Croom Helm. *48-9*

Middleton, S. (1989) 'Educating feminists', in S. Acker (ed.) *Teachers, Gender and Careers*, London: Falmer. *75*

Millman, M. and Kanter, R.M. (eds) (1975) *Another Voice*, New York: Anchor Books. *139*

Minns, H. (1985) 'Boys don't cry', *Times Educational Supplement* 5 April: 18. *37*

Morgan, C., Hall, V. and McKay, H. (1983) *The Selection of*

Secondary School Headteachers, Milton Keynes: Open University Press. *82–3, 85, 88*

Morin, E. (1971) *Rumour in Orleans*, London: Weidenfeld & Nicholson. *41*

Morris, J.G. (1981) 'The research and intelligence unit of the Scottish Education Department', *Scottish Educational Review* 13 (2): 162–6. *113*

Mortimore, P., Sammons, P., Stoll, L., Lewis, D. and Ecob, R. (1988) *School Matters*, Wells, Somerset: Open Books. *2, 25, 26*

MSC (1984) *TVEI Review*, Sheffield: MSC. *100*

Mungham, G. and Pearson, G. (eds) (1976) *Working Class Youth Culture*, London: Routledge & Kegan Paul. *45*

Murcott, A. (1980) 'The social construction of teenage pregnancy' *Sociology of Health and Illness* 2 (1): 1–23. *50*

Murcott, A. (1983) 'Cooking and the cooked', in A. Murcott (ed.) *The Sociology of Food and Eating*, Aldershot: Gower. *108–9*

Murcott, A. (1988) 'Sociological and social anthropological approaches to food and eating', *World Review of Nutrition and Dietetics* 55: 1–40. *108–9*

Murdock, G. and Phelps, G. (1973) *Mass Media and the Secondary School*, London: Macmillan. *46–7*

Nash, R. (1973) *Classrooms Observed*, London: Routledge & Kegan Paul. *23*

Newson, J. and Newson, E. (1976) *Seven Years Old in the Home Environment*, London: Allen & Unwin. *19, 20, 22*

Newson, J. *et al.* (1978) 'Perspectives on sex-role stereotyping', in J. Chetwynd, O. Hartnett and M. Fuller (eds) *The Sex Role System*, London: Routledge & Kegan Paul. *22*

Nias, J. (1989) *Primary Teachers Talking*, London: Routledge. *68*

Nilson, A. P. (1975) 'Women in children's literature', in E. S. Maccia *et al.* (eds) *Women and Education*, New York: Thomas. *21–2*

Norwich, J.J. (1967) *The Normans in the South*, London: Solitaire Books. *91*

NUT/EOC (1980) *Promotion and the Woman Teacher*, London: NUT/EOC. *81, 86*

Okely, J. (1975) 'Privileged, schooled, finished', in S. Ardener (ed.) *Perceiving Women*, London: Dent. *115*

Ott, S. (1986) *The Circle of the Moutains*, Oxford: Clarendon Press. *109*

Paley, V.G. (1984) *Boys and Girls: Superheroes in the Doll Corner*, Chicago: The University Press. *23, 28–9, 38*

Paley, V.G. (1986) *Mollie is Three*, Chicago: The University Press. *38*

Parker, H. (1974) *View from the Boys*, Newton Abbot: David & Charles. *53, 113*

Parsons, G.N. (1981) 'English literature: teachers, relevance and the "great tradition" ', *Education for Development* 6 (3): 31–41. *104*

Partington, G. (1976) *Women Teachers in England and Wales*, Slough: NFER. *80, 81*

Peterson, P. and Fennema, E. (1987) 'Effective teaching for boys and girls', in D. Berliner and B. Rosenshine (eds) *Talks to Teachers*, New York: Teachers College Press. *33*

Pilcher, J., Delamont, S., Powell, G. and Rees, T. (1988) 'Women's training roadshows and the "manipulation" of schoolgirls' career choices', *British Journal of Education and Work* 2 (2): 61–6. *92*

Pilcher, J., Delamont, S., Powell, G., Rees, T. and Read, M. (1989a) 'Evaluating a women's careers convention', *Research Papers in Education* 4 (1): 57–76. *10, 92, 98, 114*

Pilcher, J., Delamont, S., Powell, G. and Rees, T. (1989b) 'Challenging occupational stereotypes', *British Journal of Guidance and Counselling* 17 (1): 59–67. *92, 114*

Pilcher, J., Delamont, S., Powell, G. and Rees, T. (1989c) *Career Choices for Schoolgirls: An Evaluative Study of the Cardiff Women's Training Roadshow* (bilingual), Cardiff: Welsh Office. *92, 98, 114*

Pollard, A. (1985) *The Social World of the Primary School*, London: Holt Saunders.

Pollard, A. (ed.) (1987) *Children and their Primary Schools*, London: Falmer. *130*

Pollert, A. (1981) *Girls, Wives, Factory Lives*, London: Hutchinson. *106*

Powell, R.C. (1979) 'Sex differences and language learning', *Audio-Visual Language Journal* 17 (1): 19–24. *101*

Powell, R.C. (1984) 'Where have all the young men gone?', *Times Educational Supplement* 4 February: 84. *101*

Powell, R.C. (1986) *Boys, Girls and Language*, *101*

Powell, R.C. and Littlewood, P. (1982) 'Modern languages: the avoidable options', *British Journal for Language Teaching* 20 (3): 152–9. *101*

Powell, R.C. and Littlewood, P. (1983) 'Why choose French?', *British Journal for Language Teaching* 21 (1). *101*

Pratt, J., Bloomfield, J. and Seale, C. (1984) *Option Choice: A Question of Equal Opportunity*, Slough: NFER. *95*

Prendergast, S. (1989) 'Girls' experience of menstruation in school', in L. Holly (ed.) *Girls and Sexuality*, Milton Keynes: Open University Press. *65*

Ramasut, A. (ed.) (1989) *Whole School Approaches to Special Needs*, London: Falmer.

Rees, G., Williamson, H. and Winckler, V. (1989) 'The "new vocationalism" ', *Journal of Educational Policy* 4 (3): 227–44. *103*

Rees, T.L. (1983) 'Boys off the streets and girls in the home: youth unemployment and state intervention in Northern Ireland', in R. Fiddy (ed.) *In Place of Work*, London: Falmer. *4*

Rees, T. L. (1986) 'Education for enterprise', *Journal of Educational Policy* 3 (1): 9–22.

Rheinberg, N. (1988) 'The golden jubilee of test cricket in England', *Wisden 1988*, Sussex: Wisden. *117*

Rheingold, H.L. and Cook, K.V. (1978) 'The content of boys' and girls' rooms as an index of parents behaviour', *Child Development* 46: 459–63. *20*

Rich, S.L. and Phillips, A. (eds) (1985) *Women's Experience and Education*, Cambridge, MA: Harvard University Press. *120*

Richardson, B.L. and Wirtenberg, J. (eds) (1983) *Sex Role Research*, New York: Praeger. *120*

Riddell, S. (1989) 'Pupils, resistance and gender codes', *Gender and Education* 1 (2): 183–98. *64–5, 66*

Roberts, H. (ed.) (1981) *Doing Feminist Research*, London: Routledge & Kegan Paul. *111*

Roberts, H. (ed.) (1984) 'Putting the show on the road', In C.

Bell and H. Roberts (eds) *Social Researching*, London: Routledge & Kegan Paul. *111*

Rocheron, Y. (1985) Unpublished PhD thesis, University of Warwick. *50*

Rossiter, M.W. (1982) *Women Scientists in America*, Baltimore: Johns Hopkins University Press. *101*

Runciman, S. (1951) *A History of the Crusades*, vol. 1, Cambridge: The University Press. *91*

Rutter, M. *et al.* (1979) *Fifteen Thousand Hours*, London: Open Books. *2, 113*

Sadker, M. and Sadker, D. (1982) *Sex Equity Handbook for Schools*, London: Longman. *5*

Sayers, D. L. (1935) *Gaudy Night*, reprinted 1976, London: New English Library. *118*

Sayers, J. (1984) 'Psychology and gender divisions', in S. Acker *et al.* (eds) *Women and Education*, London: Kogan Page. *114*

Schneider, J. and Hacker, S. (1973) 'Sex-role imagery in the use of the generic "man" in introductory texts', *American Sociologist* 8: 12–18. *62*

Scribbins, K. (1977) 'Women in education', *Journal of Further and Higher Education* 1 (3): 17–39. *79–80*

Serbin, L.A. (1978) 'Teacher, peers, and play preferences', in B. Sprung (ed.) *Perspectives in Non-Sexist Early Childood Education*, New York, Teachers College Press, and in S. Delamont (ed.) (1984d) *Readings on Interaction in Classroom*, London: Methuen. *31–2*

Shafer, S. (1976) 'The socialization of girls in the secondary schools of England and the two Germanies', in *International Review of Education*, 22 (1): 5–24.

Sharp, R. and Green, A.G. (1975) *Education and Social Control*, London: Routledge & Kegan Paul. *23*

Shibutani, T. (1966) *Improvised News*, Indianapolis: Bobbs-Merrill. *41*

Shone, D. and Atkinson, P. (1981) 'Industrial training for slow learners', *Education for Development* 6: 25–30. *4*

Shuy, R. (1986) 'Secretary Bennett's teaching', *Teaching and Teacher Education* 2 (4): 315–24. *63*

Sikes, P., Measor, L. and Woods, P. (1985) *Teacher Careers*, London: Falmer. *68*

Simon, B. (1965) *Education and the Labour Movement*, London: Lawrence & Wishart. *114*

Simon, B. (1974a) *The Two Nations and the Educational Structure*, London: Lawrence & Wishart. *113, 114*

Simon, B. (1974b) *The Politics of Educational Reform*, London: Lawrence & Wishart. *113, 114*

Skelton, C. and Hanson, J. (1989) 'Schooling the teachers', in S. Acker (ed.) *Teachers, Gender and Careers*, London: Falmer. *73*

Smail, B. (1984) *Girl Friendly Science*, London: Longman. *61*

Smail, B. (1986) 'Girls into Science and Technology', in J. Brown *et al.* (eds) *Science in Schools*, Milton Keynes: Open University Press.

Smart, C. and Smart, B. (eds) (1978) *Women, Sexuality and Social Control*, London: Routledge & Kegan Paul.

Smith, D.E. (1987) *The Everyday World as Problematic*, Boston: North Eastern University Press. *113*

Smith, L. S. (1978) 'Sexist assumptions and female delinquency', in C. Smart and B. Smart (eds) *Women, Sexuality and Social Control*, London: Routledge & Kegan Paul. *45, 49, 59*

Smith, L. M., Dwyer, D.C., Prunty, J. J. and Kleine, P.F. (1986) *Educational Innovators: Then and Now*, London: Falmer. *2*

Smith, L.M., Dwyer, D.C., Prunty, J.J. and Kleine, P.F. (1987) *The Fate of an Innovative School*, London: Falmer. *2*

Smith, L.M., Dwyer, D.C., Prunty, J.J. amd Kleine, P.F. (1988) *Innovation and Change in Schooling*, London: Falmer. *2*

Smithers, A. and Hill, S. (1989) 'Recruitment to mathematics and physics teaching', *Research Papers in Education* 4 (1): 3–21. *69*

Social Trends 19 (1989) London: HMSO. *68*

Spender, D. (1982) *Invisible Women*, London: Writers & Readers Publishing Cooperative. *63, 115*

Sprung, B. (ed.) (1978) *Perspectives on Non-Sexist Early Childhood Education*, New York: Teachers College Press.

Stacey, J. *et al.* (eds) (1974) *And Jill Came Tumbling After*, New York: Dell. *20*

Stanley, J. (1989) *Marks on the Memory*, Milton Keynes: Open University Press. *48*

Stanley, L. and Wise, S. (1983) *Breaking Out*, London:

Routledge & Kegan Paul. *111, 113, 120*

Stanworth, M. (1983) *Gender and Schooling*, London: Hutchinson. *4, 115*

Stones, R. (1983) *'Pour Out the Cocoa, Janet': Sexism in Children's Books*, London: Longman. *120*

Stubbs, M. (1976) *Language, Schools and Classrooms*, London: Methuen. *6*

Stubbs, M. (1983) *Language, Schools and Classrooms*, 2nd edn, London: Methuen. *6*

Stubbs, M. and Delamont, S. (eds) (1976) *Explorations in Classroom Observation*, Chichester: Wiley.

Sussman, L. (1977) *Tales out of School*, Philadelphia: Temple University Press. *38, 39–40*

Sutherland, M. (1985) 'Whatever happened about co-education?', *British Journal of Educational Studies* xxviii: 155–63. *80*

Tann, S. (1981) 'Grouping and group work', in B. Simon and J. Willcocks (eds) *Research and Practice in the Primary Classroom*, London: Routledge & Kegan Paul. *40, 58*

Taylor, J. (1980) 'Choice: a male prerogative', in J.G. Morris (ed.) *Choice, Compulsion and Cost*, Edinburgh: HMSO. *99*

Tey, J. (1947) *Miss Pym Disposes*, London: Davies. *88*

Thorne, B., Kramarae, C. and Henley, N. (eds) (1983) *Language, Gender and Society*, Rowley, MA: Newberry House. *62*

Tickle, L. (ed.) (1987) The Arts in Education, London: Croom Helm. *105*

Tropp, A. (1957) *The School Teachers*, London: Heinemann. *68*

Turner, B. (1974) *Equality for Some*, London: Ward Lock.

Upton, G., Beasley, F., Atkinson, P. and Delamont, S. (1988) *The Effectiveness of Locational Integration for Children with Moderate Learning Difficulties*, Cardiff: Welsh Education Office. *10, 100*

Waldon, R. and Walkerdine, V. (1985) *Girls and Mathematics*, Bedford Way Papers 24, London: Institute of Education.

Walford, G. (1989) 'Shouts of joy and cries of pain', in D. Raffe (ed.) *Education and the Youth Labour Market*, London: Falmer. *105, 106*

Walker, D. (1986) *Gender Equality: an Effective Resource for*

Today's Classroom, Wisbech, Cambs: Learning Development Aids. *121*

Walker, J. (1988) *Legends and Louts*, London: Unwin Hyman. *53*

Walker, M. (1983) 'Control and consciousness in the college', *British Educational Research Journal* 9 (2): 129–40. *88*

Walker, S. and Barton, L. (eds) (1983) *Gender, Class and Education*, London: Falmer. *119*

Walker, S. and Barton, L. (eds) (1989) *Politics and the Processes of Schooling*, Milton Keynes: Open University Press.

Wallace, C. (1987) *For Richer, For Poorer*, London: Methuen. *46, 52*

Waller, W. (1932) *The Sociology of Teaching*, New York: Wiley. *78, 79*

Walum, L.R. (1977) *The Dynamics of Sex and Gender*, New York: Rand McNally. *14–15, 23*

Wandor, M. (ed.) (1972) *The Body Politic*, London: Stage One. *20*

Weiner, G. (ed.) (1985) *Just a Bunch of Girls*, Milton Keynes: Open University Press. *99, 120*

Weiner, G. and Arnot, M. (eds) (1987) *Gender under Scrutiny*, Milton Keynes: Open University Press. *120*

Weiner, G. and Arnot, M. (eds) (1988) *Gender and Education*, London: Open University London Region Office. *119*

Weis, L. (1989) 'The 1980s', in S. Walker and L. Barton (eds) *Politics and the Process of Schooling*, Milton Keynes: Open University Press. *5, 66*

Wells, J.H. (1985) 'Humberside goes neuter', in J. Whyte *et al.* (eds) *Girl Friendly Schooling*, London: Methuen. *82*

Whitehead, A. (1976) 'Sexual antagonism in Herefordshire', in D.L. Barker and S. Allen (eds) *Dependence and Exploitation in Work and Marriage*, London: Longman. *70*

Whiteside, M.T., Bernbaum, G. and Noble, G. (1969) 'Aspirations, reality shock and entry into teaching', *Sociological Review* 17:293. *74*

Whyld, J. (ed.) (1983) *Sexism in the Secondary Curriculum*, London: Harper & Row. *121*

Whyte, J. (1983) *Beyond the Wendy House*, London: Longman. *120*

Whyte, J. (1984) *Gender, Science and Technology: Inservice Handbook*, London: Longman.

Whyte, J. (1985) *Girls Into Science and Technology*, London: Routledge & Kegan Paul. *5, 114*

Whyte, J., Deem, R., Kant, L. and Cruickshank, M. (eds) (1989) *Girl Friendly Schooling*, London: Routledge.

Wickham, A. (1985) *Women and Training*, Milton Keynes: Open University Press. *99, 120*

Wilkins, K. (1979) *Women's Education in the United States*, Detroit: Gale Research. *119*

Wilkinson, L.C. and Marrett, C.B. (eds) (1985) *Gender Influences in Classroom Interaction*, Orlando, FL: Academic Press. *23*

Willis, P. (1977) *Learning to Labour*, Farnborough: Saxon House. *47, 48, 49, 52, 53, 54*

Wilson, D. (1978) 'Sexual codes and conduct', in C. Smart and B. Smart (eds) *Women, Sexuality and Social Control*, London: Routledge & Kegan Paul. *45, 49–50*

Winter, M. (1983) 'Remedial education', in J. Whyld (ed.) *Sexism in the Secondary Curriculum*, London: Harper & Row. *60–61*

Wolpe, A.M. (1974) 'The official ideology of education for girls', in M. Flude and J. Ahier (eds) *Educability Schools and Ideology*, London: Croom Helm.

Wolpe, A.M. (1977) *Some Processes in Sexist Education*, London: Women's Research and Resources Centre. *77, 78*

Woods, P. (1979) *The Divided School*, London: Routledge & Kegan Paul. *75–6, 79, 102*

Woods, P. (1987) 'Becoming a junior', in A. Pollard (ed.) *Children and their Primary Schools*, London: Falmer.

Zimmern, A. (1898) *The Renaissance of Girls' Education in England*, London: Innes. *81*

Subject Index